Formation of
the Analyst

Psychoanalytical Notebooks

London Society
of the New
Lacanian School

Issue 36, December 2020

Director of NLS Publications: Alexandre Stevens
Consulting Editor: Pierre-Gilles Guéguen
Editor in Chief: Janet Haney
Issue Editor: Peggy Papada
Editorial Team: Aino-Marjatta Mäki, Colin Wright
Text setting & cover design: Linda Lundin
Translator: Philip Dravers
Proofreading: John Haney

Published by the London Society of the NLS
Correspondence Address:
Psychoanalytical Notebooks, 42D Maple Street, London W1T 6HF, UK
Email: janetrhaney@gmail.com

ISBN 9781916157637

Contents

Editorial

Lacan's desire for a school of psychoanalysis went beyond Freud, beyond Oedipus, beyond the structure of "the all" and its antinomic element. This was the logic of "all men" born of a father who stands as the exception, guarding jouissance and enjoying all women. Impossibility and prohibition of jouissance are inherent in this structure, which leads to rigid classifications. Yet in the Lacanian School "there is no exception, but rather an ensemble, or rather a series of exceptions, of solitudes incomparable to each other" and as such the school is "not-all in the sense that it is logically inconsistent, and presents itself in the form of a series in which a law of formation is missing."[1]

In the "Founding Act" of Lacan's school in 1964 what is most striking is the absence of a definition of what a psychoanalyst is. Instead, the word "work" permeates the text and what is specified is the school's basic organ, the cartel. The anti-segregative, anti-didactic mechanism of the cartel provides a social link whereby everybody works together and at the same level around a project called psychoanalysis. It is the transference to psychoanalysis and to the analytic discourse, rather than an ideal, that "allows singularities to hold together."[2] Work transference encourages each member to participate actively in psychoanalysis, to think about theory and practice, and not simply to remain in a position of consuming texts and various teachings without implicating oneself, one's own question and one's own body.

The school is "the organism in which there is work to be accomplished." It is "inseparable from the training to be dispensed."[3] The contribution Lacan makes to the formation of analysts is to assert that analysts are not taught and trained by other analysts. There is nothing universal about the analytic discourse. The analytic discourse cannot be taught. Instead, analysts are formed by their own analysis, as Lacan made clear in the "Proposition of 9 October 1967 on the Psychoanalyst of the School."[4] One becomes a psychoanalyst through the experience of encountering the real through one's symptom.

Nevertheless, how to teach what cannot be taught is a question throughout Lacan's teaching: how can psychoanalysis be taught, how can a knowledge be taught to all when this knowledge emerges from the intimacy of the analytic situation where, for example, interpretation aims at a momentary act of saying and knowledge is acquired only by means of going through an experience which is singular and incomparable? How can one transmit something without falling prey to either the traps of mastery, thinking oneself as univocal, or to the snares of the university discourse, where the ideal *I* prevails?

Lacan's response to the question of how to demonstrate a formation based on the principle of self-authorisation is the pass. "The event of the pass is the act of saying on the part of a sole person, the Analyst of the School, when he puts his experience into order,"[5] when he or she testifies in front of an audience to his or her analytical path.

We are privileged to publish in this issue of the *Psychoanalytical Notebooks* a series of texts by psychoanalysts of the World Association of Psychoanalysis who have gone through the procedure of the pass and been nominated and who, one by one, tell us something about the formation of the analyst and its three pillars of analysis, supervision and the cartel (i.e. the study of psychoanalysis). Right now, in the New Lacanian School, there is a dynamic interest in the end of analysis, in the production of analysts and in the transmission of psychoanalysis itself, and this was testified to in the inaugural event on *The Pass in Our School, the Teaching of the AS*, held in Ghent, in September 2019. This was a response to the nomination of Florencia F.C. Shanahan – the first Analyst of the School to have gone through the procedure of the pass within the NLS.

The first four papers of the current issue (Laurent Dupont, "Formation of the Analyst, the End of Analysis"; Bruno de Halleux, "The Rhinoceros and the Desire of the Analyst"; and Patricia Tassara,

"Supervision" and "From Dreams to Body Event") have all been taken from presentations recently delivered in London during a series of events on the *Formation of the Analyst* organised by the London Society of the NLS. The last two papers (Florencia F.C. Shanahan, "Present"; Véronique Voruz, "Bodies Captured by Discourse") were given in online events organised by our NLS colleagues in Berlin (Lacanian Orientation in Berlin) and Dublin (Irish Circle of the Lacanian Orientation) respectively. This testifies to an ongoing interest in and desire for the question of formation in the members of our community at large.

The formation of the analyst is at the foundation of the school of Lacan. "The analytic discourse exists because it is the analysand who supports it."[6] There cannot be an analyst without being an analysand, just as there cannot be an Analyst of the School without the school. The permanence of formation of the "analyst-analysand," as Laurent Dupont puts it in the first paper of this issue, as the underlying principle of the Lacanian orientation means a continuous ascesis of working to become an analyst.

Peggy Papada
December 2020

Formation of the Analyst, the End of Analysis

Laurent Dupont

Formation of the Analyst, the End of Analysis

Laurent Dupont

Presentation given 19 January 2019, as part of the Formation of the Analyst series of events, organised by the London Society of the New Lacanian School. Laurent Dupont is Analyst Member of the School (AMS), the current president of the ECF and member of the WAP.

Every psychoanalytic institution, of whatever kind, awards the title of analyst to those candidates whom they consider, after a designated procedure, to have finished their analysis. So there is a relation between the end of the analysis and being an analyst. The formation of the analyst is, first and foremost, his or her analysis. To this Lacan will add supervision and the cartel. We will focus today on analysis because it is the central focus of training for all psycho-analytic organisations.

What Is the End of an Analysis?

For those who are oriented by Lacan, the end of the analysis implies a procedure: the pass. In 1967 Lacan formalised this procedure in the now classic text: "Proposition of 9 October on the Psychoanalyst of the School."[1] It does not come out of the blue. In 1964 he had been – according to his own expression – excom-municated from the IPA. This led him to cancel the seminar he had been preparing and to return instead to *The Four Fundamental Concepts of Psychoanalysis*: the drive, transference, repetition and, of course, the unconscious. But the title that Jacques-Alain Miller gives to one of the chapters that deals with the unconscious should make us prick up our ears. This title, "The Freudian Unconscious and Ours," is proof of a distance that separates Lacan from Freud, an autonomy. The introduction of object *a* shakes things up, and three years later Lacan will propose two titles, two nominations for analysts of his school: AMS and AS, and these are still in force today.

In the "Proposition," he specifies things as follows: "The AMS or Analyst Member of the School [is] constituted simply by the fact that the school recognises him as a psychoanalyst who has proved himself." I will not develop this, but here we have the version of the analyst at work, the one who analyses patients, who is at work in his practice, who gives supervision, who takes part in cartels, teaches, exposes his practice... etc. And "The AS, or Analyst of the School, who is characterised as being among those who are able to testify to crucial problems for analysis, at the vital point they have come to, especially insofar as they themselves are working on them or at least working towards resolving them." This often gets translated as "able to testify to the crucial problems of psychoanalysis," yet Lacan is very clear that it concerns crucial or vital points that they have arrived at insofar as they themselves are at work at or at least on the brink of solving them. It is also about being put to work, but not in a professional capacity, analysing patients, but rather as testifying *for analysis* – testifying to the logic of the cure, to its effects and to its vital points.

It seems to me that here we see a twofold logic emerging: AMS, an analyst confirmed in their practice; AS, an analyst who can testify for psychoanalysis. There is a disjunction between the practice itself, and even a didactic analysis, and the pass that testifies to psychoanalysis and its results, that is what is crucial.

For those who think they have finished their analysis, it is a question of exposing the master signifiers in play, the main drive object at stake in the fundamental fantasy, and the crossing, that is to say the cession of jouissance experienced at this crossing. But, with the very last Lacan, there is a beyond, in which it is a question of identifying what remains, what keeps reiterating itself – always and from the start – which he calls the sinthome. This is what we will explore, but before we do we must see that the question of the end of analysis, of becoming an analyst, itself has a long history.

Freud and the Rock of Castration

Freud posed the question of the end of analysis at each stage of his exploration of the human psyche. Obviously, the high point of his reflections on this topic is his late work "Analysis Terminable and Interminable."

In this text, Freud will question the very notion of the end of analysis, first in terms of its duration. The whole of the first part of this text addresses the understandable desire to want to shorten the duration of analyses. I really recommend that you read this because it is still very important for us today. It gives fundamental clinical indications and delivers a critique of the American model of analysis. On page 216, after referring to Rank's suggested means of shortening analysis, by jumping straight to the primal trauma – namely, for Rank, the universal trauma of birth – Freud says: "Rank's argument [...] was a child of its time, conceived under the stress of the contrast between the post-war misery of Europe and the 'prosperity' of America, and designed to adapt the tempo of analytic therapy to the haste of American life."

Freud used the metaphor of a fire brigade to indicate that the question of the cause does not resolve the question of the jouissance in play.

Having evoked and refuted all the reasons for wanting to shorten an analysis, he takes us down the road of being attentive to transference, and in particular to negative transference, as well as the mobilisation of mechanisms of defence by the patient, a defence against the drive, the excesses of the id and the superego or, as we would say, of jouissance. These two axes are the sign that the subject is defending himself from the point that marks an unsurpassable limit for Freud: the rock of castration "against which we see our efforts come to nothing."[2] He specifies the rock of castration as *Penisneid* for the woman, and as the refusal of femininity for the man. This led Jacques-Alain Miller to say that every fantasy is a fantasy of virility. We will come back to this.

Thus, for Freud, an analysis ends when we reach this stopping point. He proposes (without it ever having been applied) that one should have another slice of analysis every five years so as to know a little more about what is in play regarding one's insurmountable relationship to castration for someone who calls themselves an analyst.

Miller and the Rock in the Road

I propose to orient our line of enquiry with a quotation from Jacques-Alain Miller, where he says: "When you are nominated as an AS, as an Analyst of the School, it means that you have been deemed to be, henceforth, capable of continuing your work as an analysand alone. And nothing else."[3] The pass is not a guarantee, it is about putting oneself to work in a different mode. With Freud's proposal that one resume analysis every five years, Lacan's proposal that beyond the end of analysis and the crossing of the fantasy there is something that repeats, and Miller's indication that, from that moment on, one continues one's work as an analysand alone, we have various echoes of Freud's terminable *and* interminable, finite *and* infinite. It is not a question of *or*. This *and* raises the question of something finishing and something continuing.

A marvellous little book of three lectures that Miller gave in Salvador de Bahia in 1998 has just been published by Navarin with the title *L'Os d'un*

Cure [The Bone of the Cure]. I thank Ève Miller-Rose for her editorial work and Christiane Alberti and Philippe Hellebois for establishing the text. It is no doubt starting to become obvious that I am reading Lacan with Miller, step by step, and that if I read Lacan, it is because I first encountered Miller's body animating his course, his "vociferation", in order to take up his development of Lacan's work. I gave a testimony about it in the *Questions of School*.[4] For there to be a transference, it takes a body; for there to be analysis, it takes a body; for there to be an analyst, it takes a body. We will come back to this.

For these lectures, Miller begins by evoking a poem by Carlos Drummond de Andrade: *No meio do caminho* ("In the Middle of the Road"). Though it may not do the poem justice, I will give you the following translation:

> In the middle of the road was a stone
> was a stone in the middle of the road
> was a stone
> in the middle of the road was a stone.
>
> I shall never forget that event
> in the life of my so tired eyes.
> I shall never forget that in the middle of the road
> was a stone
> was a stone in the middle of the road
> in the middle of the road was a stone.

I'm not going to simply copy and paste Miller's analysis of the poem. Let's just say that there is a road and a stone, that the stone is there, in the middle, you cannot miss it, it's there. Let's also say that the road is the path of speech of an analysis and that the stone constitutes this stopping point, but also beyond. If the stone is in the middle of the path, there is a beyond of the stone. What is this stopping point, what is this stone? We will say that this stone takes various forms according to whether it is spotted by Freud or by Lacan in his first, second, late, or even very late teaching.

For Freud, the idea is that in the middle of the road there is a stone, a rock, the rock of castration which, according to Freud, has to do with "the assumption of one's sex, and not the assumption of death."[5] Why do I evoke death here? Because unlike Freud, Lacan's first teaching suggests that there is a mortification of libido. The word comes to mortify the thing. This is one of the senses of the famous Lacanian proposition: the word is the murder of the thing. When we follow the path around the stone in the middle, the Freudian stone, the rock of castration, when we follow this path taking Lacan's hand so as not to get lost, with his first teaching as a compass, we find death. Thus, if the pass had been conceived at this point in his teaching – it's not the case, I am proposing this purely in hypothetical terms – the end of the analysis at that moment would have been the assumption of death, which is how Miller describes it, and it is written like this:

$$\frac{A}{\cancel{J}}$$

To illustrate this, Miller comments on the painting that can be found on the cover of *Seminar XI*: Holbein's *The Ambassadors*. Beneath the images, beneath the prestige, beneath the fascination, beneath the shimmer of illusions, death would be the truth, unmoving and tough. The consequence of a pass oriented by the symbolic as that which mortifies jouissance would be to make jouissance a quantity to be negativised. However, it does not work like this. If the operation of the symbolic on jouissance brings about a mortification – which is the meaning of the formula A over barred J – there is a remainder. This remainder is both a condenser of jouissance and the cause of desire as it testifies to the lack inherent in the operation of mortification: the object a. This is where the second Lacan leads us – the end of analysis is no longer a mortification but a crossing. The subject is barred because of the mortification, because of the operation of the signifier, but remains articulated with this waste, this scrap, this remainder, this object, and this produces the formula of the fantasy based upon the lozenge. In the middle of the road, once you go around the rock of castration, there is a stone that allows you to take your bearings in another way. It is the object a.

Lacan, Symptom, Sinthome

In the "Proposition", Lacan proposes a beyond of the fantasy of virility, which allows access to the feminine position both for a man and for a woman. This is the famous "crossing of the fantasy." I say "famous" because, as Miller reminds us, Lacan only used this expression once. Here, again the function of the *and* is in play because what the analyst-analysand testifies to is the crossing of the fantasy *and* its beyond. "Beyond" implies that the analyst-analysand continues on his way, but it is not the same. We never step into the same river twice, we could say that we never walk down the same road twice when we do an analysis. So there is a path, a road beyond the rock of castration, and the stone, the stone in the middle of the road, is the object *a*.

Let us continue with Miller: "To be an analyst is only ever to work to become one. Finite analysis, I would say, is also infinite."[6] This is a new version of the analyst: it is not a title, it is not a function, it is a setting to work, and as such it is a version of the French expression *demain on rase gratis* – tomorrow, you'll shave for free – which is to say that it is necessary to return to one's task each time and keep working away at it once more.

Why? Why can't we say, "That's it, I am a blank slate wiped clean of jouissance, it's over. I am a psychoanalyst"? Well, we must not exaggerate, we can say that, and in fact we can say anything, we can even paint a picture of a pipe and say this is not a pipe. That's why people don't wait for the pass or any other procedure to call themselves a psychoanalyst – at this moment a psychoanalyst is a bit like Magritte's pipe; one could say: *ceci n'est pas un psychanalyste.*

Speech can give meaning to everything, it can say anything, so much so that, as Lacan puts it, "Speech *bien entendu* is defined as being the only locus, where being has a sense."[7] And if there is one thing that makes someone go into analysis, it is to find a meaning, a meaning for what is happening to him. Well, as Lacan says, this can only take place in speech, in speech as a locus. Being is made of words, *paroles*, namely attempts to make sense, this sense is given by speech. An analysis is made of speech.

The invitation to free association is not a wish to say anything, much less a duty to say something, but to say everything that goes through your head. The wager is that from this speech there will emerge an act of saying [*un dire*] that will be an event, producing a before and an after. It is therefore, as always, under transference that an act of saying can suddenly occur that will be an event in the analysis.

There is thus a double movement which allows us to see straight away that there is a twofold articulation of the Other with a capital O: first, the function of the Other as the locus of the signifier and then the Other as a body, giving a new definition of fantasy: fantasy is the place par excellence where the signifier and jouissance come together. It is a very beautiful solution because it knots the imaginary, the symbolic and the real. The fantasy is a representation, a scene in the imaginary, and also a signifying articulation where the subject of the signifier is present, plus a quantity of libido marked as object *a* that supplements it.[8]

Where the crux lies, and this is what we are going to see today, is that, in relation to the crossing of the fantasy, Lacan takes a step further by bringing out the signifier's dimension of jouissance, the endless enjoyment of sense, of meaning that each signifier calls for – a metonymy S_1 (S_2-S_2-S_2-S_2 ...), where each S_2 hides within itself what it is: an S_1. Hence Lacan's expression: a swarm, an *essaim*, which in French sounds just like the S_1 it evokes.

So here we have another occurrence of *and* – we've had: finite *and* infinite, the fantasy *and* the beyond of the fantasy (which has a little bit of Buzz Lightyear about it), and today we have: the big Other, as both the locus of the signifier *and* as the body.

Before getting to this point of identifying what in this lozenge has articulated the signifier as mortification and the signifier as jouissance, there is the process of analysis. An analysis is made of speech and operates as a reduction of speech. It is a process of reduction. The crazy liberty of free association is transformed into a taste for speaking well, the *bien dire*. Saying it well is speech that, drunk with meaning, dries out towards the *bien dire* along the road of the object *a*. Miller says this in *L'os d'une cure*.

An analysis almost always begins with a lack [*défaut*] of signification. The jouissance included in the symptom being opaque to sense, something creates an enigma or hole, leaving the subject lacking a word, a meaning, an explanation. This lack of meaning takes the turn of a request addressed to the analyst.

> You encounter a signifier whose sense you cannot understand, you go in search of another signifier so that it can be linked to the first. In other words, the signifier of transference pushes you to go and find its meaning in relation to an analyst as another signifier.[9]

We go into analysis with an S_1, in search of an S_2, and what we discover over the course of an analysis and what gets revealed at its end is that the transference is not the S_2, but the search itself.

This S_1 is what we call the symptom, it is the support of the demand, the signifier of the transference. "An analysis associates a symptom with a knowledge, and through this usually gets rid of this symptom."[10] This knowledge, included in the very function of the symptom, is itself at the centre of the transferential relation, establishing a double knowledge. First, the symptom is the sign of something to be discovered. This discovery is already included in the symptom. To discover it is to discover the knowledge included in the symptom and, at the same time, to produce a knowledge for oneself – S_2. Then there is a second knowledge, this one supposed to the analyst, of knowing how to read a symptom, of knowing how to produce the interpretation, of knowing how to lift repression. This knowledge remains supposed as the analyst does not use it. Hence the fact that the analyst does not remove the option of S_2.

However, today, where the address is more often made to a psychologist than to a psychoanalyst, this request is often accompanied by a request for instructions about "how to...?", so that interpretation doubles as a user manual. In responding to the demand for both meaning and a set of instructions, the psychologist plugs up the open space of meaning, leaving the unconscious completely outside the work that takes place, and reduces the encounter to the idea of an exchange about demand, communication, intersubjectivity – so many trinkets offered up to anxiety.

The first paradox of analysis is precisely this lack of meaning that produces transference, because the long-awaited S_2 is kept in abeyance. The transference is therefore based on the enigma that the subject is to himself. The end of the analysis takes place once all the meanings and all the constructions developed and dreamt up [*élucubrées*] around this central point of the unspeakable (where the part of opaque jouissance included in the symptom testifies to what is most singular in each person) have been exhausted.

There is, then, a beyond of meaning which allows one to reach that point which, if it cannot be said, can be felt through the effect of an act of saying [*l'effet d'un dire*] or an effect of saying, of saying well – an *effet de bien dire*. In his "Preface to the English Edition of *Seminar XI*", Lacan proposes the following: "When the esp of a lapse (...) has no further meaningful scope (or interpretation), only then is one certain of being in the unconscious."[11] To be in the unconscious is to be beyond language, it is to "pierce through the wall" of language.[12] What is aimed at in the language borne by speech is no longer the swarm produced by the S_1. It is, as Lacan says in *L'étourdit*, what happens when the reading of the session lacks the reference point and so makes the radical solitude emerge (the silence, the non-articulation). This act gives rise to an event in the empty retroaction, which makes the inexistence of the Other suddenly emerge in a flash of realisation [*dans un aperçu*].

Well, the same goes for the formation of the analyst. The break, the equivocation, the jaculation, aims at resonance and relinquishes the reason of meaning. "It is part of the formation of the analyst to know how to identify this propositional reduction, in other words to know how to capture the constant."[13] Why aim at resonance? Because what resonates is the body, it resonates in the repetition of the signifier's first strike on one's enjoying body, the first bite, the first impact. This impact implies a second mode of enjoyment, a second jouissance, a jouissance from the encounter with the signifier, the one that iterates, the one that infiltrates, the one that interferes. "The first element involved in the process of reduction is *repetition*."

This gives us an idea of what we are dealing with: "The Freudian Unconscious and Ours" and what we are grappling with today – the symptom vs. the sinthome. The Freudian unconscious is the unconscious that interprets and that harbours the part of meaning to be found. Ours has a non-sensical dimension, which is on the side of the empty reference, the letter, the trace, the mark. It is the same for the symptom vs. the sinthome. The symptom is Freudian, it means something, or rather, as we say in French – it wants to say something, to be heard with the equivoque that falls on the word "wants": on the one hand, it insists, it has something to say, it is a ciphered expression of the drive and analysis can decipher it. Here there is the revelation of the repressed meaning and the removal of the symptom. From this point of view, the symptom is a formation of the Freudian unconscious. And yet something insists beyond meaning, there is a persistence, an iteration; the lifting of repression is never complete. "The *sinthome*, unlike the symptom, is never removed."[14] The sinthome belongs to the real unconscious, it includes the real, the real of what it concerns. An analysis carried out to the end aims to touch, to reach this bit of real, this area where the esp of a lapse no longer has a meaning, where the unconscious no longer interprets or is interpretable, it is the thing itself, the trace, the mark.

I propose that we make a distinction between repetition and iteration. Repetition is the interpretable part of the symptom's jouissance, it obeys the function of meaning that seeks to emerge according to a thrust or impulse [*poussée*] that implies joui-sense. Iteration is part of real jouissance and as such is uninterpretable by meaning – opaque to meaning, as Lacan says: it is the sinthome.

This double movement is very well summarised by Miller: "Let's introduce a little dialectic here between the stone and the road. It is because there is the obstacle that there is repetition, but it is because there is repetition that the obstacle comes into view."[15]

This means that we must first go through the elaboration, the lucubration, a long analysis in the name of the S_2, before we can reach this point at which, if it escapes meaning, if it escapes speech and being, according to the proposition advanced by Lacan in "Joyce the Symptom", it does not escape repetition in the form of iteration.

Iteration is both repetition and convergence. Something repeats beyond meaning and reveals itself through its very repetition and, at the same time, a convergence takes place. On the road we cannot help but go towards the stone. It can be done in a spiral, in detours, but if you want to go to the end you must learn to spot both the repetition and the lines of convergence. "I will call the second mechanism, after repetition, *convergence*. The cure will in fact show that the subject's acts of saying all converge towards a fundamental *énoncé*, a fundamental statement." Miller goes on to say, "The statement towards which this convergence leads is that of a *master signifier* – a signifier that has become master of the subject's destiny."

The Subject and the Parlêtre

Iteration can also be revealed by what the subject avoids and spares himself from saying, over and over again. In repetition there is presence, in convergence there are lines of signifiers tending towards a point, and in avoidance only absence. "The network of impossible successions that repetition always avoids, as if the most important thing to repeat was the avoidance." On the road of analytic speech, there is the stone that cannot be avoided and, to reach it, the analyst trains himself to spot, over and over again, repetition, convergence and avoidance – three terms which in their usage contain two aspects of interpretation: an effect of meaning experienced *in* one's body, and a trace outside meaning, experienced as coming *from* the body, the iteration of the first encounter with the signifier which is forever traumatic. It is an encounter that separates the body and the being in the experience of jouissance, thereby making the body Other. "The analyst's attention must not allow itself to become fascinated by repetition and the repeated and constant convergence, but must also focus on the repetition of absence, avoidance, circumvention, which constitutes precisely a stumbling block for the subject" – a stumbling block, or as we say in French, a *pierre d'achoppement*, in other words, a stone.

That is to say that there are no provisions for the encounter between bodies. Bodies exist, One all alone. So, there is language. Language is what allows human bodies to encounter each other, at least it allows us to believe that they do. The little human, an enjoying substance, is One, all alone, that is to say without Other. This jouissance is One all alone

– not solitary, alone in its radicality. The encounter with the Other – that is to say, with language, thus with what there is of the Other inasmuch as there is something of One [*il y a de l'Un*] – comes to make a hole in this body of One all alone. To make it enter into one is not possible without there being first some kind of '*faire avec*' or 'doing with' this unprecedented encounter with the Other of language that has come to bite into our bodies.

There is thus One, all alone. The encounter with the Other produces a real which introduces a subtraction; the One is subtracted from the One, and what remains is the zero and the enigma or hole of the signifier. Here the Other emerges as S_1, but beneath this S_1, there trails [*traine*] the trace of this first fundamentally traumatic encounter. This trace is an inarticulable defence against this real. Suddenly, all the clinical categories that we encounter, whatever name we give them, are only defences against the real. And the relation to the Other comes to be marked by this underside of the S_1, letter, trace, mark ... "We can thus formulate that, in analytic experience, there is a hiatus, a fault, a rupture of causality between the signifying articulation – knowledge as it is represented on the graph – and libidinal investment."

The S_1 will or will not be articulated with an S_2, producing a second time of jouissance, one in which the whole apparatus of the formations of the unconscious, symptoms and delusions emerge... Which led Lacan in his very last teaching to say that with regard to this One jouissance, with regard to the sexual non-rapport, everything is make-believe, semblant, everything is a delusion with regard to the real at stake there.

An analysis pursued to its end is an analysis that goes back up the signifying chain to the point of making the subject's relation to the S_1 emerge in the undressing of being that leads the subject on to the point of finally experiencing the inexistence of the Other, namely $S(\cancel{A})$.

Conversion: "The most important thing is not the signifier's effect of mortification on the body, but the fact that the signifier is the cause of jouissance. The signifier has an impact of jouissance on the body, which Lacan calls a symptom."

This long path of the signifying chain will lead us to the beating heart of the question, the object *a* insofar as it constitutes an intimate link with the Other, while at the same time separating us radically from it. For if the object *a* is located in the Other, it is only located there through being a production of our own. Through its fantasmatic articulation, it allows one to believe in the encounter, in the meeting, which is far from being without interest.

For the encounter only takes place if one believes in it without being duped by it. The end of the analysis, as proposed by Miller in "The Unconscious and the Speaking Body", is not therefore the mortification of jouissance by the symbolic, but the discovery that the signifier itself is a source of jouissance, that speech itself is jouissance. There is enjoy-meant, *jouis-sens*, and an additional jouissance below the bar, in the voice, in the very body that speaks – it is not the voice, it is not without the voice, it is the body in the voice. This is how one can become adept at pointing out its trace in the analysis. This will be beautifully demonstrated by Miller in his course on vociferation, which he borrows from Lacan. The end of the analysis is not the end of meaning, fantasy and jouissance. No, it is about logically grasping this know-somehow with the real, namely this initial encounter of a body substance with the unprecedented jouissance of the encounter with the signifier, which engages a double movement, a logical iteration of this jouissance, and a metonymical displacement that can be tracked in the productions that follow, and which can be reduced in analysis by the way of the signifier.

> The connection between the signifier and jouissance must be conceived theoretically: the libido's attraction by the signifying articulation, the signifier plus libido, in other words the libidinal investment of the signifier, and also the separation between signifier and libido, the signifier minus libido, which Freud calls disinvestment.

So in this version of the *and* of the signifier, and the effect of meaning and jouissance, the subject is barred because of the mortification of jouissance brought about by the symbolic, and it then recuperates some of it through the object a – as the formula of fantasy shows – but for the parlêtre, the jouissance of the body is linked to the signifier as its consequence. As soon as we include the body in the analytic equation, we move from a minus to a plus. The subject, $\not S$, is marked with a minus by the symbolic, through the operation of castration, the product of which is the object *a* which serves as the means to deny it, plugging it up in the substitutive enjoyment that it offers; but the parlêtre is marked with a plus, as the living body is alive with the enjoyment of the signifier taken in speech. "Lacan brings the living body into psychoanalysis at the same time as the jouissance of speech: the parlêtre enjoys by speaking. Symbolisation doesn't just annul jouissance, it also preserves it."

As a result, we obtain a new *and*, the barred subject, the result of a mortification of jouissance by the signifier *and* the parlêtre, the living body enjoying. On one side we have the want of being and on the other "the subject plus the body."

In the pass, this double movement implies not believing too much in the story we are telling ourselves, as pass testimonies are so many fictions, since they only account for the part of the signifying chain that has to do with history. Of course, having dried it out, having purified it, each AS has reduced it to a name, a letter, a core, it is "a discourse in which the semblants clasp a real, a real in which one can believe without adhering to it."[16] The names become reference points that allow us to read the logic of the testimony so that they lead us beyond, where having lost their brightness, no more a beacon or tag, no more meaning, at the threshold of the inexistence of the Other we catch a glimpse of the radical solitude of the person giving the testimony. The solitude teaches us about the uncoupling of the signifying chain, there where the Other, the treasury of the signifier, always aims to offer us another one, one more with which to plug the first S_1 with meaning, forming the couple S_1-S_2. There is a concatenation of the signifying chain in analysis, bringing it back to that point where neither the metonymic slippage nor the metaphor operates any more. At this point the Other emerges as: $S(\cancel{A})$, the body insofar as it does not lend itself to being caught in the definitions of meaning, but in the most opaque part of the symptom's jouissance.

Here again, do not be too fascinated. Catching a glimpse is not to install oneself there, no one aims to wander in *the uninhabited realms of being*. I recall the following sentence by Miller which gives this lecture its orientation: "When you are nominated as an AS, as an Analyst of the School, it means that you have been deemed to be henceforth capable of continuing your work as an analysand alone. And nothing else."[17] You are thus the analyst-analysand. It's just that at this moment one can no longer be unaware of knowing it. To engage in the procedure of the pass, to want to testify, first to the passers [*auprés des passeurs*], then in the escabeau of the pass,[18] is to confront the experience of the event of saying [*l'événement du dire*], saying by giving one's testimony.

"Isn't turning one's symptom into an *escabeau* precisely what is at issue in the Pass?" There is, in the pass, in the public testimony, an event of saying, a body that speaks. This is how Jacques-Alain Miller proposes this moment of testimony as a demonstration that we could call a de-monstration – namely, something that shows itself to be hollowed out, in the hollow of what speech cannot deliver, but which the act of saying, insofar as it includes the body, allows to pass, or not. There is no guarantee in the testimonies, just an event, carrying a speech which may or may not constitute an event. "It still falls to the analysed parlêtre to demonstrate his savoir-faire with the real, to demonstrate how he knew how to make an art object, and how he knew how to say it, to say it well" and he adds: "an act of saying [*un dire*] is a mode of speech which distinguishes itself in constituting an event."

Why do acts of saying, why do signifiers bite so deeply into our bodies, leaving an indelible trace, and why this one rather than another? We could consider that all these words, these sentences, the fantasy itself, are only reticulated on the basis of the first point, the One of the first encounter of an enjoying body with the signifier. This introduces a double register of jouissance, the One jouissance, and jouissance as an iterative trace of this encounter, which remains forever singular for everyone. This point cannot be said, it is aimed at and circumscribed. The testimonies are fictions, the names of semblants. And yet, there are effects. Effects in the body of the speaker, effects in the body of those who listen. Not all the testimonies have the same effects on everyone, not all the analysts of the ECF testify to the same effects.

These effects *en-corps*, in the body, attempt to say, not the impossible real, but the singularity of each which rests, not on the *reasoned* elements of the demonstration, but on the *resonance*, the *réson*, always already there, that the encounter with an analyst allowed one to hear.

Thus, the event of saying resounds throughout the analysis, from this transference that gathers its substance from the gap opened in meaning and catches hold of the body beyond speech, to the testimony of the AS, the Analyst of the School, which becomes – in the very speech through which the testimony is delivered – the resonance of the saying that marked an event, and an event of saying in itself.

We will stop here, for today, on this *and*: finite *and* infinite, the crossing of the fantasy *and* its beyond, and also for us today, the subject *and* the parlêtre, that is, the want of being *and* the body. Thus, the analyst-analysand is the one who remains awake to this living body that escapes the definition of meaning, making of this sinthome the fulcrum of the analyst's desire. What is this desire? It is to lead each person who comes to see him, and who thus sets off down analysis's road of speech, to the stone, the stone in the middle of the road, which testifies to what is most singular in oneself.

The formation of the analyst is to conduct his analysis to the end, to the crossing of the fantasy and the circumscription of this irreducible jouissance that iterates. This new *ça-voir*, then, brings forth the dimension of pursuing alone, not the deciphering of his unconscious, but the *savoir y faire avec*, the knowing-somehow or knowing-how-to-do with this point of real that was initially encountered, always as traumatic, but from which each parlêtre has produced his own singular *savoir y faire*. It is on the basis of this *savoir y faire* – this knowing-somehow – that the analyst's desire, which is also always singular, can be discovered and articulated.

Translated by Philip Dravers

The Rhinoceros and the Desire of the Analyst

Bruno de Halleux

The Rhinoceros and the Desire of the Analyst

Bruno de Halleux

Presentation given 4 November 2018 as part of the Formation of the Analyst series of events organised by the London Society of the NLS. Bruno de Halleux is a psychoanalyst practising in Brussels; he is a member of the ECF, NLS and WAP.

In relation to the formation of the analyst, the expression "the desire of the analyst" has always appeared to me to be somewhat murky. I will try to develop it with reference to what Lacan says about analysis, supervision and the pass. In exploring these elements, I will share my experience as a former Analyst of the School (AS) and as a therapeutic director in an institution.

Introduction

I'd like to thank Philip Dravers for the invitation to come here to the London Society to speak about the formation of the psychoanalyst. He sent me a text by Éric Laurent where this point has been worked through with the rigour and seriousness typical of his style. The text, "The Logic and Surprises of Supervision at the Time of the Parlêtre," principally concerns supervision and is correlated with the formation of the analyst. I recommend that you read it. You can find it in *The Lacanian Review*, No. 2, 2016.

The formation of the analyst is a very special and complex subject. Its complexity prompts me to present it here in fragments, as if I were sewing a patchwork.

University?

No university can provide this kind of formation. We can't find any formation of the analyst in a university, it is not possible. Or, if you do find one, then it's not serious... You can't have a degree or diploma to be a psychoanalyst from any university. The formation is not reducible to a knowledge that we can find in books.

In *Histoires de ... Psychanalyse*, a radio series that Jacques-Alain Miller gave in 2005,[1] he asked if it would be possible to imagine an exam that could judge one's ability to be an analyst. "What could it be? Of course, you cannot analyse someone in public. The exercise of psychoanalysis is reserved for the most intimate confidence, the trust that someone gives to an analyst. No one else could interfere in this relationship." May we imagine that the interpretations of the analyst are collected and constitute examination material? It would be absurd and nobody has tried it. The quality of the psychoanalyst cannot be attested to by a public examination.

What the analyst says is valid only in the speech relation between the analyst and his analysand. An analytical interpretation is not convincing in itself. What matters is not its content, its abstract meaning, but its function in the moment when it is uttered and the unpredictable effects that it arouses in the one who receives it in the context of this very special relationship.

That's the reason why Lacan told us that a formation of the analyst doesn't exist. "There is no formation of the psychoanalyst, there are only formations of the unconscious."[2] So the only way to get a formation if one day you want to become an analyst is to begin an analysis for yourself.

In the formation of the analyst, there is something that cannot be transmitted. Something untransmissible. So how can we teach something that cannot be taught?

There is no automatism in the analytic formation, there are no mechanisms to learn in order to become a psychoanalyst.

Lacan defines the psychoanalyst as the result of his or her own analysis. One is an analyst when one has found, via analysis, the exit from one's own impasses. That is the first point. The formation of the analyst requires a personal cure. And the cure requires at least a symptom. Without a symptom – without something odd, strange, problematic in your life – there is no possibility of beginning a cure.

Some time ago, I received a young lawyer who wanted to switch from his profession to that of psychoanalyst. He asked me what was the financial commitment of the psychoanalyst, how many years of learning, and if it was worth it and so on. I just replied that if he wanted to be an analyst, he had to begin a cure and I didn't know how long it would take because the unconscious doesn't know time.

This is why it is impossible for a psychoanalyst to identify himself with any model. Lacan makes it clear that one can become a psychoanalyst only by renouncing it from the point of view of identity. There is no identity for the psychoanalyst. The psychoanalyst is the result of his own cure. As such, no two analysts are alike. As everyone is a singular person, each analyst follows his own analysis and is the result of his own cure.

This consideration turns the analyst into a perpetual analysand. There is no permanent AS. In a certain way the psychoanalyst is always at work with his unconscious.

An Anecdote from Lacan's Practice

One day, Lacan received a young analyst in supervision. The guy told Lacan the complex case of a patient at the beginning of his clinical experience. Lacan listened attentively and replied: it's perfect! The young analyst was delighted to get this encouragement from Lacan. Perfect! Imagine, a real compliment coming from Lacan!

The next day, however, the analyst discovered that the diagnosis he had given to Lacan was wrong. It was not a hysterical neurosis, as he had first thought. It was in fact an untriggered psychosis – what is now called an ordinary psychosis. Then he went back to Lacan's office and said: "How is it possible that you congratulated me on my erroneous diagnosis?" Lacan answered: "Oh, you have found out! Well done, I'm glad you have now understood."

This anecdote shows a clinical modality of learning for this young analyst. Lacan does not interpret the statements of the young analyst. He interprets his utterance.

The first movement of the analyst is to act as a rhinoceros. He interprets from his certainty of being an analyst who is right in deciphering the formations of the unconscious, but what he doesn't see is precisely that the interpretation must not only be reasonable in its deciphering – it must also resonate. This is a word game in French because reasoning is said in the same way as resonate: *raisoner – résonner*.

That's why, in his text "The Logic and Surprises..." Laurent tells us that the rhinoceros has become the animal emblem for the formation of the analyst. Both modes of interpretation correspond to two different times in Lacan's teaching. The first one is where the analyst operates in the name of reason, the signifier, the formations of the unconscious. The interpretation could be written with this matheme: $A/\mathcal{J}$, the Other over barred jouissance, the jouissance which is withdrawn, extracted. The second one is that of the object, of what Lacan called the register of the drives, or, to say it in a different way, the register of jouissance. Here the matheme could be written: $A \rightarrow$ Jouissance. The big Other, the signifier, is cause of jouissance.

On page nine of *Seminar XXIII, The Sinthome*, Lacan gives us a definition of the drive: "The drives are the echo in the body of a fact of saying." This definition joins the register of the signifiers (a fact of saying) and the register of the body. The incarnation of a signifier in the body.

Definition of the Desire of the Analyst

The desire of the analyst as defined in *Seminar XI* is different from the definition given at the end of Lacan's teaching. At the start of this talk, I said that the desire of the analyst had always appeared to me to be somewhat murky. I'll try to explain to myself and to you what the desire of the analyst is, and how it can emerge.

In *Seminar XI*, the words of Lacan are clear about the desire of the analyst: it is a desire to obtain absolute difference, a difference that comes when the subject, facing the primordial signifier, comes for the first time to be in a position to subject itself to it.

What does it mean? Isn't it an aporia, a logical difficulty? The word "difference" means that there are two things to compare. One thing is different from another. In other words, the difference is always relative between an S_1 and an S_2, a first signifier and a second one. But Lacan uses the word "absolute" about the difference. How can one understand it? "Absolute" means there aren't two things to compare.

There is another definition of the desire of the analyst when we take into consideration the second time of Lacan's teaching. It is a time where the unconscious is taken not as the result of chains of signifiers in which one of them is repressed. That was the time of the transferential unconscious, where there was a chain of signifiers, and the unconscious corresponded to the repressed signifier, and this signifier was the one to be deciphered. In the second time of Lacan's teaching we find what Jacques-Alain Miller calls the real unconscious, which is in opposition to the transferential unconscious.

We can find this new definition of the desire of the analyst in a text by Miller presenting the theme of the 2014 WAP congress in Rio: "The desire of the analyst is the desire to reach the real, to reduce the Other to its real and to liberate it from meaning."[3]

Two definitions: one about absolute difference, on the way to find one's primordial signifier, an S_1, a signifier without S_2, a signifier with no comparison because it is an S_1, a signifier alone...

A signifier alone! Here again we have a new difficulty: what is a signifier alone? What is a signifier without the second one, without the S_2? This is not easy to understand. If I want to understand the meaning of the S_1, I need a second signifier which gives a signification to the first one. But if there is not a second one? How to understand? If you understand the signifier alone, then the risk is that you are wrong. Understanding always requires at least two signifiers. In our lives, we usually compare ourselves with the other. We always compare things, qualities, those we have and those we don't have... So how are we to understand "obtaining the absolute difference"? And how can we understand the primordial signifier?

The other definition is the desire to touch the real, to reduce the Other to its real. From the first one to the second one there is a movement where the accent moves from symbolic to real.

This second definition is as murky as the first one. What does it mean to "reduce the Other to its real"? I guess that it's close to what Lacan said in *Television* when he compared the analyst to a saint. A saint doesn't do charity: a saint is not someone who wants your happiness, he is rather someone whose reply puts you in front of yourself. He starts to be the waste: he un-charits, or, as it is translated in the English version of *Television*, "his business [is] trashitas," not caritas. In French the verb is *déchariter*. The psychoanalyst's business is trashitas. He puts the analysand subject in front of his own real.

The Desire of the Analyst in a Cure

An analysis can have a diversity of fates. A subject may start the analysis with dreams of changing the world, a belief in the idea that he will be able to free himself, to come out of his defences, out of his inhibitions, out of his neurosis and to live fully a choice of love and of work.

But after a number of years, broken, tired after a long and interminable analysis, he gets used to what he became, he must accept his limits, his castration, his impotence. He is finally disillusioned. It has to do with his symptoms. You have to accept that "you are that." No more, no less. You have to accept that the world is as it is. This conception of psychoanalysis is cynical because, by not asking too much, by finding an "arrangement" with his work and with his wife, the subject maintains a small jouissance. He turns into a cynical hermit who from now on knows that he should not ask too much from the other, that nothing will ever change, and that since the world is like this, there is no Good, Beauty or True. He must accept it and line up obediently.

Well, I think that the desire of the analyst is what comes to hinder this cynical fate of the analysis. Éric Laurent gives a wonderful conclusion to what love becomes in the dignity of psychoanalysis. He says:

> Psychoanalytical wisdom does not lie in knowing that everything falls into a grey area and that when one loves, one can be a little bit aggressive, [...] it is to know whether one loves or whether one hates and to be consistent with the decision that one makes. It will not necessarily be eternal, it is not a eulogy of sublimation but is, in any case, a lauding of decision. [...] It is a conception of psychoanalysis where one does not pick up one's chips and leave the table, but where one continues to play with the Other, and continues to expend oneself without counting the cost; and there, love can be at the rendezvous.[4]

I've encountered the desire of the analyst at different moments in my analysis. When I was in the last part of my analysis, I went to my sessions but had nothing more to talk about. And if I tried to say something, the analyst cut short any attempt at narration. How can I speak about "nothing to say"? The sessions were a moment of pure presence where I could only enter his office, greet him and leave without a word. I felt, however, that each of my sessions was essential and I would not have missed any of them.

We can read this position on the second level of the graph of desire. The second level corresponds to the will of a subject in the articulation of his speech. But this will is played on the vector of a pure enunciation, a pure call of being. The matheme of this discourse is written ($\$ \lozenge D$), which is the subject marked by the signifier which is related to a demand that has been exhausted by all the demands of the subject during his analysis. This subject remains marked by the avatars of this demand. This place of the matheme which Lacan notes as the drive inscribes the subject of the signifier which relates to the nothingness of the demand. Silence of speech that correlates with the pure presence of being. This point, which I had arrived at in my analysis, was marked by this need outside meaning, this urge that I felt to go to see my analyst to tell him ... nothing! During these sessions, there was a body event that I did not understand and which was repeated each time I evoked the father, or one of his figures. Just when I was talking about the father or one of his figures, tears came to my eyes even though I did not feel any sadness. It was a strange experience. I asked my analyst what could explain this phenomenon of tears.

He replies: "Tears are very mysterious."

This intervention – tears are very mysterious – remains enigmatic for me. This answer from the analyst seems to me to be on a level other than the current meaning of interpretation. Once, an interpretation was given to a meaning with an S_2, the next signifier. Here, though, the words of my analyst do not open onto a new meaning. They do not produce a new meaning. Rather, this statement is disconnected from any S_2 because it is looping back on itself.

Words cannot say things of the body. Tears touch the body, from which something of jouissance must be extracted. This interpretation indicates the desire of the analyst, it aims to free the subject from meaning. There is nothing more to say!

The Desire of the Analyst in an Institution

I said that I would speak about the formation of the analyst from my experience as therapeutic director of Antenne 110. This institution is not a place for the analytical treatment for children, but it belongs to the field of applied psychoanalysis. It is a clinical practice inspired by psychoanalysis. Antenne 110 is known in lot of places in Europe and in Latin America and is often cited because of the originality of its practice, something Miller has called "a plural practice," or, in French, *la pratique à plusieurs*.

I formed myself as an analyst at Antenne 110, but without a clear conception of this formation while it was happening. Very often, the psychology trainees from the university would ask me for a training during the psychological sessions. I replied to them that the best formation for them was to participate in the workshops with the children.

In parenthesis: Éric Laurent has recommended that all analysts should do an internship in an institution to find the right measure for their narcissism! I agree: it would be necessary for some of them.

I would like to add that Antonio Di Ciaccia created this institution as an effect of his own analysis with Lacan, and that it was supported by the desire of Lacan. The success of the plural practice is secretly related to the desire of the analyst supported by the therapeutic director. So I reread Antonio's text about plural practice[5] to understand where the desire of the analyst is and how I've been formed by my practice with autistic children.

The first teaching I received was this one: I was beginning my practice in Antenne 110 and I received an indication from Antonio about something I told him about a child. This child was autistic and didn't speak at all. Once, I told Antonio what the child had wanted to say. "How do you know that?" he asked me! And then he reminded me of Lacan's warning that it is impossible to know what someone wants to say when he does not say it. Then I was thinking: "Oh, did the subject mean that? So how do I know?" What is certain is that this has not been said. The analyst is not guided by his ideals or prejudices. Giving value to the act of saying is the foundation of the Freudian discovery.

A second lesson: Antonio Di Ciaccia describes the function of the therapeutic director not as the one who knows, but the one who preserves a central space – an empty space, a void, in the heart of knowledge, and this allows for every child one by one. It is the clinical verification of the Lacanian axiom and its consequences: an autistic child is in language even if he doesn't speak. There are two effects of occupying this place: a destitution of each from an objectifying knowledge (rather like an a priori relation to non-knowledge), while at the same time staying completely responsible for the act of the teacher (the one who intervenes clinically).

Di Ciaccia writes that the function of the director is similar to the plus-one in a cartel; he is the one who pushes the subject to say, the one who pushes the subject to elaborate.

As mentioned above, Miller's definition of the desire of the analyst is as follows: "It is the desire to reach the real, to reduce the Other to its real and to free him from meaning."

Well, this expression "to free the Other from meaning," to free the subject from meaning, is one of the central functions which the therapeutic director has to assume. And in this operation, the desire of the subject, the desire of the civilised analysand (as Laurent puts it), the desire of the teacher, will always be more awake.

To wake up the subject, to free him from meaning, gives the subject unbelievable joy. But to gain this, to arrive at this loss of meaning, to be formed as an analyst, we have to follow the experience of an analysis until the end.

Supervision

Patricia Tassara

Supervision

Patricia Tassara

Presentation given 29 June 2019 as part of the Formation of the Analyst series of events organised by the London Society of the NLS. Patricia Tassara is a member of the ELP and of the WAP.

In the Act of Foundation of the Freudian School of Paris,[1] in 1964, Lacan talked about supervision. There he referred to the experienced analysts, the didacts, saying that supervision was concerned with "the interior problems of the outcomes of the didacts." This means that supervision is necessary during the treatment of the analyst but also beyond the end of the treatment. Analysis has an end, but supervision is endless. Lacan situated the entrance to supervision but never situated an end of it.

Three years later, in the "Discourse at the Freudian School of Paris" (October 1967), he refers to supervision as the "correction of the desire of the analyst."[2] As F. Rueda, one of my colleagues in Spain, said in a congress in Paris about the real: This 'correction' sounds like the subjective 'rectification' Lacan mentioned in "Direction of the Cure."[3] Therefore, we can put these elements into a series: the entrance into supervision and the correction of the desire.

The demand for supervision takes place when the subject is exceeded by his act. The important word here is "subject". Because the analyst does not operate as a subject, a divided subject, from that position he will always be exceeded. He operates from the position of object *a*, in order to make the semblant of object *a*. Supervision is the tool to recapture the position of the semblant of object *a*, in order to empty the space of the cause of the desire of the analysand.

Lacan described two moments of supervision: first moment, when he referred to the analysts that initiated their practice, he named them: rhinoceros. We have to imagine a rhinoceros inside a shop full of porcelain ornaments. In the second moment, supervision consists in finding the equivocation that can liberate the sinthome, learning the use of a creative word, but also the use of silence. In his course *Being and the One* (2011), Miller says that in supervision we learn to acquire the power of the word so that the analyst's word can be creationist. We also learn to be quiet.

There are no norms or rules to tell us about our position as analysts. Psychoanalysis is not guided by any aim of transparency, standard operators or norms to follow, because there is an irreducible opacity of the real. As Éric Laurent says, the analyst is not in the place of a universal Other of good faith, not in the place of a father. It takes time until a practitioner stops believing in transparency, in the Name of the Father or in the guarantee. The analysand is a believer who has to consent to the fact that the era of shadow will never be illuminated completely.

In the pass, the passant presents his own case in the pass device. The pass is necessary to "isolate the 'lie in the real' to allow the strangeness of supervision to appear in its proper light,"[4] says Laurent. So the perspective of the pass is an important orientation to consider.

What is supervised is the analyst's position and his act. Supervision is required when the position of the analyst is an obstacle in the orientation to the real. Not only what returns always to the same place, but what returns where the subject does not perceive what concerns him.

The real is what always returns to the same place. In this sense, jouissance is the most real and impossible to dialectise. Sometimes jouissance burns, burns bodies, even books that speak of it, as happened to Freud's books under Nazism. In *Seminar XXIII*, chapter 8, Lacan says fire is the real, "the real sets fire to everything but the real is a cold fire. The fire that burns is a mask of the real. The real must be sought elsewhere, on the side of the *absolute zero*."[5] This mention of the absolute zero is an attempt to separate from the Freudian conception of libido as a quantum, linked to the scientific positivism of the era in which Freud was immersed. Lacan adds that the real is what guides us. Therefore, it is a fundamental dimension to understand not only our concepts but also the practice and experience of psychoanalysis.

In the "Proposition",[6] Lacan says the real provokes its own misrecognition, and its systematic negation.

We are not free from this, even in our psychoanalytic institutional functions.

As in analysis, supervision is a device that revolves around a real. This does not mean that it is not possible to make clear the coordinates of a case, or think about the structural orientation. It is the possibility to interrogate what is the obstacle at the level of the practitioner's position in the direction of the cure. Making use of supervision allows the practitioner to grasp the difficulty, making an effort to separate from impotence and be oriented by the real. The real is what preserves us from standardisation; therefore, ours is a customised supervision.

In *Seminar XXIV*,[7] Lacan says knowledge is the unconscious, is the effect of signifiers, and then he makes a difference between *savoir faire* and *savoir y faire*. *Savoir faire* is what we understand as know-how. If in supervision we pretend that the supervisor will give us a know-how, it means we believe there's a know-how as a solution, then we will confront ourselves with impotence and a failure of knowing.

Savoir y faire is what is expected at the end of analysis with the sinthome. It is necessary to traverse the neurotic mental debility and accept that it is always impossible to say everything. The *savoir y faire* is an operator, and it can be translated as 'to deal with', which is different from a simple 'know how' (to do). In this seminar Lacan says there's a not-know-how-to-do with knowledge: "*L'homme ne sait pas 'faire avec' le savoir.*" That's his mental debility. He adds that he himself is not an exemption in this, because he has to manage with the same material that inhabits all of us – language. *"Savoir y faire est autre chose que de savoir faire – ça veut dire 'se débrouiller'."* This mental weakness is what we supervise in order to disentangle from it.

We supervise the inhibition to act, the excess of meaning in the case, the use of knowledge as a defence against the real, or when body events appear in the analyst. Supervision is an ethical duty for the psychoanalyst of a school. It produces singular effects in the analyst, and therefore, in the direction of the cure of his analysand.

There Are No Rules but Styles of Parlêtres

It is possible to undertake supervision with your analyst, with another analyst or with more than one analyst. Nothing is pre-written. It depends on the one by one and on transference. In the "Direction of the Treatment", point 4, Lacan says that the more interested the analyst is in his being, the less sure he is of his action. Analysis is a treatment that aims at dis-being. The pass testimonies are an excellent example of this aspect, they show us how the parlêtre could do something different with his being, with the position in his life that makes him suffer, e.g. being the phallus of the Other, completing the Other. Psychoanalysis goes from being to existence, the existence of the One, *Il y a de l'Un.*

In his 'Overture' to the *Écrits*, Lacan refers to style as the man himself and wonders if it is the man we are addressing. Finally he says: it is the object that answers the question about style. Style is the style of the object, the remainders of jouissance that resist universal logic. It is the singularity of the sinthome.

Supervision Does Not Save Us From Loneliness

Lacan talked about the loneliness of the analyst. He did so in the "Founding Act": "I hereby found – as alone as I have always been in my relation to the psychoanalytic cause – the École Française de Psychanalyse" (which shortly thereafter became the École Freudienne de Paris).[8] There's always a structural loneliness that the subject does not want to know about, he defends himself from it, and does so, for example, with the imaginary idea of belonging to a group.

When loneliness is properly treated in analysis, the bond with others works better. The more we work on our jouissance, the better we can stand the jouissance of others. The school is necessary because the position of the analyst is solitary. The bond with others, around the hole that a school is, is sustained by the work of transference, which is necessary to make psychoanalysis go forward. It is the only way to deal with the real in the interior of the school. A supervision can examine the conditions of the act, but the analyst is always alone in front of it.

Supervision and Knowledge

The effect of a supervision can help the practitioner to reduce the superego, linked to the structural hole of knowledge that sometimes produces a position of infatuation as a defence against the inherent hole in knowledge. During analysis, in every session, we go through the horror linked to the lack of an ultimate signifier that will say something about the real. The desire to know is what is found in the end of analysis.

In the "Discourse à l'École freudienne de Paris" Lacan says the unknown is arranged as the framework of knowledge. The parlêtre has to consent to the real, to the impossibility of covering every enigma with knowledge or signifiers. Knowledge is a long trek, that's why in the "Proposition" Lacan said that the knowledge we have, after studying many hours, days, months, years, is necessary, but this knowledge has to be kept in reserve when we receive a patient. It is the only way to leave the necessary emptiness, in order to listen to singularity.

It's the productive *docta ignorantia* Lacan took from Nicholas of Cusa, a thirteenth-century German philosopher and theologian. In opposition to crass ignorance, *docta* refers to a wise ignorance, which is situated in the juncture between knowing and not knowing. This is the best analytic position from which to analyse and supervise. Only then will this operative function give place to the new that is to come.

From Dreams to Body Event

Patricia Tassara

From Dreams to Body Event

Patricia Tassara

Testimony of the Pass presented in English on 5 October 2019 at the London Society of the New Lacanian School. Patricia Tassara is a member of the ELP and of the WAP.

Dreams were fundamental in my analysis. They were an effect and key instrument of the transferential unconscious and I used them until the end, let's say, until the parlêtre could arrive at the real unconscious that marked the end of analysis.

To arrive at this point, it was necessary for the parlêtre to be a believer – to believe in the unconscious knowledge, to believe that the symptom meant something, to believe in the power of words. Let's say that I believed in the existence of *The* Virgin, *The* mother of the maledictive gaze.[1] The necessary lie of this fictional belief covered the void that was found in the end.

The symptom arose with difficulties at the level of the body image, a position of phallic jouissance linked with the gaze that made an obstacle to the feminine. Analysis helped me to traverse the ravage of the maledictive gaze that had left the parlêtre in a position of melancholy.

The transference work from the unconscious interpretation – always searching for the missing meaning – transmuted into the real unconscious towards the central void of language, with the body event. The parlêtre could finally arrive at the limit of interpretation, "the limit to the autistic monologue of jouissance."[2] With the approach to the feminine position the body event emerged.

I will present a series of dreams that show changes in the position of the subject and its jouissance, showing how the body event emerged when the fantasy – formulated as: The mother crushes the woman – was traversed and the parlêtre encountered the void of S (A̸), the true void that Lacan mentions, the void crossed by an infinite line. This is the void whose limit cannot be found, whose depth cannot be plumbed.

Finally, given that we will also be holding a Cartel Study Day in the London Society of the NLS this afternoon, I will finish with a comment about my experience of working in cartels.

An IPA Interpretation

In adolescence, I went to my first consultation with an IPA analyst. In the first session, I drew a family sitting at the table, ready to eat. I could not finish the mother's face, repeatedly rubbing it out. She was the one that was not happy in the drawing. The analyst highlighted this. In another session I said that I felt "I couldn't fit in the class." The analyst asked: What class? I answered: "my school class of girl friends."

The signifier "class" had an effect. I realised it also meant economic class. As I belonged to a wealthy family, which I supposed to be wealthier than my friends', I thought that was the reason for my problems. It was the interpretation of the parlêtre but also of the family, which avoided the subjective responsibility for discontent by putting the responsibility on money.

I was sent to this analyst because I felt different, isolated and sad. I could not share the school breaks with others, staying in the classroom alone. Let's say that the analyst had in her hand the main clues to direct the treatment: a feminine sadness, the impossibility of forming a class of women, and finally the orientation of anxiety towards the real. But in the IPA they do not take into consideration the importance and logic of the real and the feminine position as Lacan developed it from the seminar *Encore*. Thus analysis was not possible.

I had a dream. I was sitting in front of a big gorilla. He was calm, staring at me. The subject was suddenly surprised by a phallic jouissance. I spoke about that surprise but unfortunately the interpretation of the analyst was purely Oedipal, and did not respect the semblants. She said: "The gorilla is your father!" After that, I didn't go back. This interpretation could not read the adolescent emergence of jouissance, the object gaze, the body concerned, or the enigma of femininity.

The Full Mirror

Many years later, in my Lacanian analysis, I had a fundamental dream, which I have developed in previous testimonies. I can reduce it here to the malaise of the gaze of a complete Other, *The* Virgin, the mother figure that petrified the body of the woman I was. As I said in my first testimony, I went to analysis because of the anxiety of being pregnant, which meant I was going to be a mother myself.

After the birth of the child, I continued feeling anxious and sad, but something new appeared, I began feeling ugly, no longer attractive to my partner nor myself. I had difficulties finding the right clothes to get dressed. Nothing fit properly. The mirror never returned the "good shape" to me. The mirror image returned the mother's face to me, with her maledictive gaze. Let's say that the mirror was too full of imaginary reflection.

During analysis, the work on this dream could empty the mirror, making it "a surface where no glimmer of meaning comes to be inscribed."[3] This dream allowed me to put the "good shape" of the symptom to work in analysis, a symptom made of signifiers: sad, ugly, mother and the jouissance of the object.

For many years, I worked on the difference between mother and woman. I was also able to discover the power of the object gaze in my treatment. I had always sought to be looked at by the Other, so as not to be petrified by the maledictive gaze. I was searching for a loveable look. In this seeking, the Other was always consistent. Another version of the fantasy isolated by the work of analysis was the subject getting itself looked at: ($ ◊ a).

The demand of the Other was something mortifying. Sadness, tears, the melancholic position were the symptomatic envelope of the hysteric.

Analysis let me talk about a complete figure: the mother, the virgin, the *cocotte*, the intelligent female friend... These were the signifiers the parlêtre used to border the impossibility of saying *The* woman. They were a means to "half-speak of her."[4] The maternal gaze, *male-dictive* (*maudit*), a gaze that was said-wrong (*dit-mal*), where speech and gaze converge, was also a male gaze that inflated hysteric masculine identification with phallic jouissance killing desire. Analysis was the attempt at well-saying (*bien dire*) even though the *bien-dire* can never be all said. This phallic position, which pretended to say all, and the drive to see all, that made an obstacle of the feminine, could be traversed in analysis.

A Dream Trembled

Years passed. I felt a lot better – my practice, my marriage, my son, my participation in the school – a good image had been found. I decided to finish analysis and went to the procedure of the pass after a dream that, I thought, marked a conclusion.

I dreamt that the house was trembling. I was standing under the door frame of my room and my son under his. I told him to hold on to the frame, and said: "Don't worry, it will *pass*." There was no anxiety in that dream.

I was not nominated. The cartel answer was a very good one, but I could not read that I was still in the mother position! The house was trembling, without anxiety: the semblants were trembling but it was not an end of analysis. The feminine was not approached. But it was a good therapeutic end.

The Unsaid Pass Dream Did Not *Pass*

During that first pass, I had another dream, between the first and second meeting with a female *passeur*. I dreamt I was driving a car. My small son was sitting in the back. Suddenly the car started falling down a sort of huge cliff. In panic, I turned my head back to look at my son. When I saw his face of terror staring at me, I woke up! This nightmare was so strong, so difficult to bear, that the unconscious immediately repressed it. I could not speak about it to the *passeur*. I could only return to that dream some years later, when I returned to analysis.

Loneliness

The encounter with a new anxiety and melancholia, due to a divorce and the encounter with an imaginary loneliness, made me return to analysis. It was the anxiety of the feminine. This second period took nine years more. The anxiety disappeared quickly and the parlêtre began to talk from an Other position, a more feminine Other. I could approach a loneliness with the symbolic Other that accompanied me in the transference, the only way to approach the real loneliness of every parlêtre. The loneliness of the inexistence of the Other. The loneliness of jouissance as One. A One alone that cannot be put in relation with anything, *Il y a de l' Un*.

The Body Trembled

Near to the end, the body trembled twice. It was without anxiety, without thinking, I just *waited* and it *passed*. I had no words to say it, and did not want to force myself to fill that event with sense. I just said: I'm alive! The session was cut with no more words.

During this last period of analysis, contingency had a fundamental effect on the parlêtre. I was concerned in my analysis and decided to take it as far as I could. The encounter with the real produced important effects to arrive at the end. Let's say that the parlêtre finally consented to the encounter with the real without its past defences. I will give an example: I went to a museum, and suddenly saw a painting that captivated me. When I read the title of the painting I thought: "I was cured of this!" The effect was a surprising separation from the melancholic envelope of sadness and mortification. The painting was E. Degas's *Melancholia*.

The body lightened!

What remains is a movement of the body. I like to move, travel to different school events, and I find the encounter with colleagues very vivid.

With patients I can wait with a productive silence, without obstructing them with knowledge.

Although my style is quick, now it is without precipitation.[5] This is the way I put the sinthome-hinge to work in the school.

The Cartel Sinthome

Lacan invented the cartel when he put the real at the

centre of the formation of the analyst. Cartels are organised according to a Borromean logic around a central void of knowledge. The school has a central void, the absence of an answer to what an analyst is, a void that makes us work and link to the school by the hinge of its main tool, the cartel. The politics of the sinthome functions as an orientation, given that there is an encounter with the real and singularity in every cartel.

It took me some time during analysis to understand the importance of the treatment of my symptomatic position with knowledge. I had to consent to the fact that the knowledge that I could capture in cartels was "detached pieces" of knowledge.

Cartels are not very comfortable, they dis-comfort us a little, as analysis does in every session. In this sense, it's not necessary to be friends to work in a cartel, because a cartel is not a group. It is not a bond between one and all. It is a one-by-one bond that prevents the school from functioning like a church.

Cartels are an "anti-didactic machine", they are anti-beatitudes and anti-sufficiencies.[6] This is why the plus-one is not a teacher, nor does he have all the answers. He is not a psychoanalyst who interprets or supervises cases in cartels. Supervisions have to be done in privacy and be paid for.

When the plus-one is situated or situates himself in a hierarchy, he is confused with the One of the exception, the dead Father with whom the others identify.

In these last years, I belonged to different cartels participating in flash cartels before school events and online cartels. I also participated in the pass device cartels and, after my nomination, for the first time I was called on to be the plus-one in two NLS cartels. I accepted to work in a different language than mine. This made me think that we suppose that we understand each other in the use of a language. But psychoanalysis is a separation from the mother tongue, from the belief that we understand the language of the Other. The mother tongue is what we know. But it is also the jouissance that we ignore, that speaks through our body, what is most extimate to us. In this sense, every language is Other, even our own.

As plus-one, I'm careful that there is no appropriation of an effect of attraction to the three years of functioning as an Analyst of the School, because this could silence the desire and singularity of the other members of the cartel. The plus-one has to be aware of the permanent effects of homogeneity in order to allow heterogeneity to prevail.

It is also important to elucidate any crisis in cartels. This could be seen in any new changes of work, of meetings, of frequency, of absence etc. It is necessary that a cartel produces a cession, a ceding of jouissance in each cartel member to work and arrive at some production. Productions are desirable and expected by the school, but not compulsory. I discovered that sometimes a cartel production appears a few months after the cartel was dissolved. Others are produced during the cartel time.

Cartels are sustained by the absence of the sexual relation: there is no harmony. It is the void of the sexual relation that echoes in each participant, including the plus-one. Each cartel puts into play a singular void made by the style of each participant. And if this void is put to work in the transference to the school, it will become productive.

Analysis allowed me to be a poor leader as plus-one, more freed from the pressures of the superego. Trying to know-how to do with difficulties, because the real always emerges. Just as in analysis, working in a cartel is a unique experience, an experience of the parlêtre where the body is concerned.

From Dreams to Body Event

Present

Florencia F.C. Shanahan

Present

Florencia F.C. Shanahan

Paper presented at an online seminar 24 October 2020, organised by the Lacanian Orientation in Berlin. Florencia F.C. Shanahan is an Analyst of the School (AS), member of the Irish Circle of the Lacanian Orientation (ICLO), NLS and WAP.

Words, profits of a quarter of an hour plucked
from the charred tree of language,
between good morning and good night,
entrance and exit doors
and entrance of a corridor going
from nowhere to nowhere.
We turn and turn in the animal belly,
in the mineral belly, in the belly of time.
To find the way out: the poem.
To tear away the masks of fantasy,
to drive a lance into the nerve center:
to incite the eruption.
Words, phrases, syllables,
stars which turn about a fixed point.
Two bodies, many beings
that find each other in a word.
The paper is covered by indelible letters,
that no one said,
no one pronounced,

that have fallen there
and blaze and burn up and die out.
Poetic justice sets fire to fields of disgrace: there is
no room for nostalgia, the ego, the proper name.
Everything must give way
before these incandescent eagles.
Every poem is realized at the poet's expense.
Octavio Paz

In March of this year, in a climate of stupor, disbelief and anguish, I wrote a short text published in LRO, entitled "Modes of Presence."[1] I did not include a definite article that could totalise these modes. Modes of a presence that is not-all. The question of the voice interrogated me from before, as well as the question of interpretation. This was the topic that we were working on in the NLS at the time of the beginning of the pandemic, in preparation for an annual Congress that was not going to be, and which left an empty place.

I will try to let myself be oriented by this place, by what "did not take place." After all, is this not one of the ways in which Freud and Lacan conceive the unconscious – what has not happened? I will also try to let myself be guided by some of the questions raised in the introductory text of the *International Fall Seminar* in Spain, with our colleagues of the Escuela Lacaniana de Psicoanálisis (ELP), a seminar which also could not take place, and which we hope will happen in the winter. This text was written for that occasion. But, in a rather mysterious way, it found a different and unexpected destination, it found another use, and thus I am here in Berlin presenting it to you.

In the introduction to the text inviting people to this ELP event, it was a question of putting to work the issue of the "massive virtualisation of life," "the universal digitisation that displaces everyday life to the support of the screens," "the massive intrusion of the technical object into experience." These are some of the ways of naming what prompts us to interrogate "the foundations and analytical principles" in our schools, insofar as "one of [the school's] requirements is to debate the conditions of possibility for the analytic experience, in times when civilisation manifests clearly the increasing degree of its impasses."[2]

There is something of this that is not new. This conversation has occupied us for more than twenty years. We did not have to wait for the confinement imposed by COVID-19 to try to put the good questions to work. Especially for those in our psychoanalytic community who apply psychoanalysis to the fields of education and mental health, this is the question they ask themselves every day: how to apprehend the mutations produced in contemporary subjectivity and how to account for the incidence and effectiveness of analytical discourse ... even now, again, still?

However, it seems important to me to also say that the question of *presence*, of the meeting of bodies, of "bodies captured in discourse,"[3] is not limited to the problem of the conditions of our practice.

For instance, for years now all objects have been removed from school playgrounds. They pose too high a risk of accidents and lawsuits. During breaks, teachers watch so that children do not run too much. And that they touch each other as little as possible, since nowadays almost nothing separates physical contact from interpretations of harassment. This of course has the consequence that a ready-made destiny for sexual and aggressive drives is offered prior to any contact, that is to say, an interpretation of what the presence of one's body introduces in the encounter, pre-empted as abuse, in any of its forms. Needless to say, teachers cannot touch children. They cannot punish them, but they also cannot comfort them or contain them with recourse to the body.

Another example: in an institution that assists minors in vulnerable situations, therapists must carry out therapy sessions with the door wide open. It's the protocol. It is transparency and its tyranny: seeing it all, recording everything, becoming a witness before the victim emerges (or perhaps precisely because of it, the victim emerges right there, finding a being – being abused – constituting and localising itself by means of such a gaze).

So-called mindfulness is introduced in all imaginable areas of life. On the official website of the Irish Ministry for Health, for instance, the public is recommended to practice it daily, with the following indication: "Being aware of the present moment can help you enjoy the world around you more. It is achieved by freeing yourself from the past and the future." School programmes have incorporated it as part of their curriculums, which as we know has – at least in Anglophone countries – been plagued for years with cognitive-behavioural techniques.

In an already classic text, Jacques-Alain Miller states that "Lacanian practice plays its game, above all, in relation to the new *reals* to which the discourse of hypermodern civilisation testifies,"[4] and whose principle is the rise of the object to the social zenith. The noise of the world multiplies itself just as the worlds we inhabit multiply themselves when what commands is the object and not the Name of the Father.[5] Silence no longer finds its guarantee in any heaven (cf. Blaise Pascal), and this is why the analytic experience continues to bet, through the collective mode that Lacan gave it – his school – to constitute a refuge and a base of operations. But unlike the twentieth century, this refuge and base of operations no longer works against the "discontent" in civilisation, the malaise created by the renunciation of the drive imposed by culture on the individual, but on the contrary, against the push to "wellbeing" incarnated by capitalism in its alliance with technology.[6]

But the *present* that is a condition for psychoanalysis as a discourse and as an experience is not the present of "full consciousness" (mind-full-ness), the present as commercialised in the industry of self-esteem, which leaves the subject at the mercy of the inner voice of the commandment of jouissance,[7] of the demand for more, of injunctions like "Anything is possible" or "Just do it!", which lead inevitably to destruction. On the contrary, the present at stake in psychoanalysis is a present sustained on the unconscious, a present that finds its support in the supposition that the unconscious constitutes and in the real that it involves.

Present. Does one need to make the signification of *gift* resonate there? "Speech is in fact a gift of language," Lacan writes, "and language is not immaterial. It is a subtle body, but body it is."[8] Caught up in images, injured by the symbol, eroticised in the transference, those words by which our body has been and is affected come into analysis on condition that the analyst becomes the "hard object" against which one becomes "pure speaker [...] Body parasitised by speech."[9] The presence of the analyst is, in his action of listening, a condition of speech, insofar as this presence remains, says Lacan, discreet:

> ...I believe that his presence is initially implied simply by his listening, and that this listening is simply the condition of speech. Why would analytic technique require that he make his presence so discreet if this were not, in fact, the case? It is later that his presence will be noticed. In any case, the most acute sense of his presence is tied to a moment at which the subject can only remain silent.[10]

The analyst's silence means that he is silent instead of responding.[11] This is the ABC of psychoanalysis, since the subject can only be identified in language by losing himself there as an object. The presence of the analyst thus founds the field of the unconscious as loss, there where his speech founds the unconscious as knowledge.

That is why Lacan, when he deals with the presence of the analyst in *Seminar XI*, refers to the expression "cause of the unconscious."[12] Cause that is circumscribed at the end of the analysis and is embodied in the singular desire that drives the function that is its product: the desire of the analyst. The object *a*, the point where the subject is separated from the signifying chain, "allows us to imagine what can be of a desire for which no being is the support."[13] Cause as a hole that is bordered by literalising the object that gave it its fixity in the fundamental fantasy, from which one separates oneself and which is finally mourned. This is a crucial question in order to be able to think what could be a *presence* that is not sustained by any kind of *being* (and, in particular, not sustained by any kind of *being an analyst*). A presence that then has the chance to constitute itself as the foundation of the analytical act. What could that act that we call interpretation be?

Last February, on the threshold of the pandemic, I wrote as follows for the NLS blog:

For Lacan, interpretation only forms a binary with the body as presence. This is one of the reasons why analysis is not possible unless analyst and analysand meet in the flesh. This does not mean, however, that the analyst interprets with his body, but rather that he interprets not without his body. There is no body to body in analysis. The topology proper to the analytic act is articulated to the poetic function, to 'the *moterialism* which in its centre closes around a void.'[14] [15]

The analyst, when there is an interpretation, embodies this void, that is to say, he embodies the non-rapport, the non-symbolisable part of jouissance, as J.-A. Miller puts it. In this way, the analyst redirects the subject to the first *absence*, which is, paradoxically, the *presence* of the opaque jouissance that singularises him, the One without an Other.

The interpretation that has an impact on the economy of the *parlêtre*, of the speaking being, is not the encore interpretation, but the interpretation *in a body* and *of a body* [*un-corps* and *en-corps*]. "An act of saying raised to the level of an event"[16] can then give access to a new use of the signifier that acts on the symptom and extinguishes something of it.

My analysis ended on the production of a new signifier. This signifier emerged in the place of the name that I had believed the Other had not given me. It was also the place I had believed that I did not have in the world. This belief sustained the not wanting to know about the impossible adequation between name and cause.

Today I conceive the presence of the analyst as this silence which, in act, constitutes itself as a saying, and which goes against both the chatter of the unconscious-knowledge and the muteness of the drive. In this silence the *absence* that is desire and the *presence* that is the unspeakable living, are realised at the same time.

The voice at stake here has nothing to do with speaking. It is not the voice of the sonorous register.

> It is the part of the signifying chain that the subject cannot assume as "*I*" and which is subjectively attributed to the Other [...] a *charge* of jouissance that cannot be integrated in the signifying chain [...] The voice comes to occupy the place of what is properly unspeakable for the subject[17]

and which, if castration has operated, was lodged in the field of the Other. Therefore, "one does not use the voice, the voice inhabits the language."[18] In my case, it was necessary for the analyst to incarnate that voice in order for it to be incorporated at the moment of separating myself from the analyst's presence, in a topology that required making a "ring of the hollow that is the void at the centre of one's being."[19]

If we can say that the analyst's position is akin to the feminine position that one consents to at the end of an analysis, it is because it is a position that leaves the place open for the unexpected (which can go from surprise to horror); it makes room for what stumbles, for what does not work. The position from where the analytic act can be supported is one that admits the opacity that inhabits each word and welcomes the mark of Otherness that the event of the body is, both in the presence of the Other and in solitude.

I shall conclude with a small childhood anecdote that arose in me while I was writing this. I must say that I never related it in my analysis, even though it was not forgotten.

My early days in school, as a child, confronted me with many enigmas about how the world worked and about what my place in it could be. Rather, it was the response that I found in my way of introducing myself to the other that often got me into trouble, and which I can remember today with tenderness. At the beginning of the day the teacher "took the roll." In alphabetical order she would say the names of each pupil to confirm attendance. When hearing one's name, one had to raise one's hand and say "present". This irritated me. I did not understand why it was not enough to be there, why it was not enough for the teacher to see us. Saying the word was necessary. Assuming the voice in that body. Then one day, when I heard my name I shouted: "absent!" It was an instant of great laughter for everyone, except for the teacher, who had no sense of humour whatsoever.

Bodies Captured by Discourse

Véronique Voruz

Bodies Captured by Discourse

Véronique Voruz

Originally given as a talk 26 September 2020 to an online event organised by the Irish Circle Lacanian Orientation (ICLO) in preparation for the NLS Congress, *Bodily Effects of Language* (22-23 May 2021, Ghent). The question posed for this particular seminar – *How do we work with the speaking bodies of the subject of contemporary civilisation?* – revealed a subtle difference from the Congress theme and gave rise to this presentation. Véronique Voruz is a member of the London Society, the NLS, the ECF, and the WAP.

Introduction

I am grateful to Florencia Shanahan and the ICLO Bureau for inviting me to open the year's work on the theme of the next Congress of the NLS, "Bodily Effects of Language." This opportunity to speak to you today led me to reflect on the title of the Congress (itself extracted from Jacques-Alain Miller's lecture series published under the title *Lacanian Biology*) and on the title under which you invited me to speak, "Bodies Captured by Discourse." The discrepancy between the two led me to reflect on the way in which the theme was taking shape for me. A distinction has to be made between the subject of civilisation and the speaking bodies we encounter in our practice.

On the one hand, we have bodies that are captured by the discourse of civilisation; in this sense, the subject is transindividual. On the other hand, language – and how we encounter it – has bodily effects that are singular to each speaking being. This second dimension of the question echoes Lacan's response to Marcel Ritter:

> It is because he is born of this precise belly and not another – he is born from a being, whether or not they desired him, and simply as a result of this mere fact he is situated in a certain way within language – that a speaking being finds himself excluded from his own origin.[1]

I will try to develop both aspects of this question, starting with the subject of civilisation, which must be distinguished from the speaking being.

With Freud

Freud first formulated the hypothesis that the structure of civilisation produced subjective effects, especially in the register of libidinal economy and symptomatic formations. Human beings are affected by the discourse of the civilisation they live in, and Freud tried to reconstruct the matrix of civilisation on the basis of what he learned through his practice. He noted the prevalence of feelings of shame, guilt and remorse in subjects whose lives provided little obvious cause to account for such intense feelings. This led Freud to posit real and fantasised parricides, and also to bring to light the infernal logic of the superego in *Civilisation and Its Discontents*. In this text, which we studied together during lockdown,[2] Freud offered psychoanalysis as a therapeutic path destined to provide a way out of what he perceived as an impasse of civilisation. Let us summarise: civilisation imposes a renunciation of drive satisfaction, or *Triebverzicht*. During his course the *Banquet of the Analysts*, on 4 April 1990, Miller says that the renounced jouissance is then separated off as excess jouissance, which is what Lacan calls object *a*, but that it returns to feed the superego. Although Freud postulates that the ethics of a civilisation, or the superego of culture, is a therapeutic endeavour internal to civilisation, it fails because the renunciation demanded by ethics continues to feed the superego, which is a modality of enjoyment of the renounced drive. "The growing impasse of civilisation can be referred back to the perpetual movement of the superego."[3] We can note, in passing, that in Freudian metapsychology, the symptom is also a way of enjoying the renunciation of jouissance:

A symptom is a **sign** of, and a **substitute** for, an **instinctual satisfaction** which has remained in abeyance; it is a consequence of the process of repression.[4]

We will return to the symptom later. But for now, let us concentrate on the impasses facing the subject of Freudian civilisation. There can be no renunciation of jouissance that does not feed the superego, for even if it feeds the symptom, the superego "knows" that the symptom is a way of enjoying the prohibited satisfaction in another way and will "punish" the subject. Freud offers psychoanalysis as a means of escaping this impasse: by lifting repression, the subject can deal with this instinctual conflict at the conscious level and avoid the return of the renounced drive satisfaction in the guise of the superegoic drive. I restate this here for the logic of my argument: Freud wants psychoanalysis to address, beyond a patient's singular issue, the impasses experienced by the subject of civilisation. This requires a precise theorisation of these impasses in order to orient ourselves in what we hope to achieve, to be precise about the libidinal stakes, in the forms that the impossible takes.

With Lacan

In his "Proposition" of 1967, Lacan picks up on *Civilisation and its Discontents* and, somewhat ominously, proffers: "When psychoanalysis will have surrendered in the face of the growing impasses of civilisation..."[5] Lacan, too, positions psychoanalysis as a response to the impasses facing the subject of civilisation. What are these impasses for Lacan? We know that he inverts the Freudian proposition that we use the unconscious as a hermeneutic device with which to interpret politics. In *Milanese Intuitions*, Miller states that Freud "analyses collective formations as formations of the unconscious having the same identificatory signifier and the same cause of desire."[6]

According to this thesis, politics can be related back to the unconscious, both being structured by the "instance of the father", repression of jouissance, and identificatory satisfactions. Instead, Lacan proposes that "The unconscious is politics," which is a development of his previous statement that "the unconscious is the discourse of the Other." In other words, the unconscious is an effect of the signifiers and the discursive logics that are at play in any given civilisation.

The extreme plasticity of the libido that Freud discovers is taken by Lacan to its fullest consequences: there is no set channel for libidinal investment. Freud, when reconstituting the matrix for the subject of civilisation, resorted to myth (Oedipus Complex, Totem and Taboo, Eros and Thanatos). Lacan, for his part, reduced myth to structure.[7] Lacan proposed that the matrix for the subject of civilisation could be written as a matheme; we know it as the four discourses. It is an ordering – three signifying elements plus object *a* – that does not rely on meaning to formalise an interpretation of civilisation. The four discourses are themselves an interpretation that can be heard as "truth is dead" – the age of the unconscious as truth is over. We can read the discourses as ways to formalise the structure of civilisation at given times.

The discourse of the master is contemporary with the Freudian period. In this discourse, jouissance is forbidden to the subject, who nonetheless recuperates a form of enjoyment via the fantasy. This allows the subject to enjoy a fantasised relation to a prohibited jouissance, to a lost object – it includes a barrier to enjoyment in reality.

The discourse of the university had taken over by the time Lacan delivered *Seminar XVII*: it refers to the proliferation of knowledges that are powerless to regulate jouissance and whose truth is simply an injunction to "continue to know." There is no barrier.

The rise of feminism inspired Lacan to write the discourse of the hysteric, which points to the truth of the two previous discourses: the master cannot enjoy his body, and the knowledge of science is impotent.

As already noted, Lacan and Freud posit psychoanalysis as a response to the impasses they perceived as besetting the civilisation of their time. Lacan then introduces an unprecedented discourse, that of the analyst. It is an interpretation in response to the would-be revolutionaries who sought to overthrow a master that was no longer the master of the game. His wager was that a new discursive logic could produce a new kind of subject, specified by de-identification and a new kind of plus-de-jouir singular to each.

With Miller

Miller continues the work of precisely situating the impasses of civilisation. The analyst's mission is, he says, to respond to such impasses. He provides us with two interpretations of the subject of hypermodern civilisation; he reconstitutes its matrix in the same manner that one reconstitutes the unconscious as the matrix of truth effects, jouissance effects and subject effects for an analysand. Let's go through these interpretations and see how they can orient us in our practice.

The first interpretation takes place in the intervention Miller made in Milan to the SLP in 2002.[8]

Miller argues that the not-all has replaced the logic of exception as the matrix for the subject of civilisation. To put it briefly, where an exception to the set once acted as a limit to jouissance, we now have a limitless set, "a developing series, without limits and without totalisation," a multitude of speaking bodies connected via the internet – mobile, flexible, ungraspable, precarious, not identified according to Freudian modalities. What are the consequences with respect to jouissance, given that our question for today is: "How do we work with the speaking bodies of the subject of our civilisation?" The logic of exception, the structure that underpinned the myth of the Father, entailed transgression as a modality of jouissance and made the limit exist in the action of transgressing it. This is beautifully explained in Foucault's "Preface to Transgression,"[9] his contribution to a homage to Bataille. By contrast, the logic of the not-all implies that a limit is not given, it has to be found, one by one. The regime of jouissance is no longer that of transgression, but that of limitlessness. This is why we are today having to deal with a clinic of excesses, addictions, etc. In his final course, *L'être et l'Un* (2011), Miller took his observation to its fullest consequence. Whereas Lacan had introduced feminine jouissance to specify a modality of jouissance that could not be treated by the phallus (or measured), Miller affirms that feminine jouissance is the regime of jouissance per se. The question then becomes one of learning how to work with this limitless jouissance, which can be devastating for many of the subjects we encounter in our practice. It is a jouissance that responds neither to the phallic signifier, which itself ciphers jouissance (*Aufhebung* on the symbolic plane), nor to object *a*, which makes jouissance countable.[10]

The second interpretation takes place two years after "Milanese Intuitions", in Miller's intervention at the WAP Congress of 2004, published as "A Fantasy". In this text, Miller proposes that Lacan's hypothesis of the analyst's discourse as the other side of the master's discourse is defunct, and that there is instead a convergence between the analyst's discourse and the discourse of civilisation. Here's a short extract from this text:

> And we could say – if we consider that the relation between civilisation and psychoanalysis is no longer a relation of one side to the other side – that this concerns rather the relation of convergence, that is to say that each of these four terms remains disjoined from the others within civilisation. The surplus jouissance commands; the subject works; identifications fall and are replaced by the homogenous evaluation of capacities; at the same time knowledge of different kinds is busy telling lies and yet makes headway nonetheless.[11]

Recall the statement in *Radiophonie* in which Lacan refers to the rise of object *a* to the social zenith. In the discourse of the analyst, the analyst causes the desire of the subject and puts the subject to work producing his identifications (S_1) and knowledge (S_2) about the truth of his position. In the discourse of civilisation, it is the plus-de-jouir that commands the subject to "enjoy"; the subject works himself into the ground, identifications are replaced by endless self-evaluations, and knowledge has the declared status of a lie, fake truth, semblants.

For example, identity politics in its current form attests to the failure of identification to suture the movement of the lack of being, the lack of being that animates the quest for an appropriate identity that would be recognised and validated by the Other. Instead of master signifiers representing a subject for other signifiers in a stable fashion, we see the emergence of continuums, spectrums, and intersectionality.

As for S_2, knowledge does not function in the manner of unconscious knowledge interpreting the irruptions of the real unconscious, making it true [*faire vrai*] in the process. We live in the era of fake news, the manipulation of public opinion, the relativism of discourse.

Finally, when it comes to the relation between $\$$ and *a*, which, in the discourse of the master, is impossible except in the guise of the fantasy, there is a relation at the level of the real. At one point in *Banquet of the Analysts* Miller asks himself what has become of civilisation and its impasses at the time of capitalism. He notes that the discourse of the master previously limited the circuit of the superego by introducing an impossible, by permitting a production of, and a separation from, excess jouissance. There is a bar (usually written like this: //) between the subject and excess jouissance in the discourse of the master so that this discourse corrects the impasse of civilisation by stealing the slave's work. The satisfaction derived from *a* only occurred at the level of the reality of the fantasy. But capitalism did away with this safeguard, introducing a connection between *a* and $. Miller defines this as the "triumph of the impasse specific to civilisation ... civilisation's path today shows that surplus-enjoyment does not merely sustain the reality of the fantasy, but is about to sustain reality per se. A reality that has become fantasy."[12] This is attested to by manipulations of reality: genetics, body augmentation, etc.

What does it mean to say that there is a convergence between the discourse of the analyst and the discourse of civilisation? In his lecture "A Fantasy," Miller said "We might say that, in civilisation, these different elements are scattered and that it is only in psychoanalysis, in pure psychoanalysis, that these terms are organised into a discourse."[13] As noted above, each of the four terms in the discourse remains dissociated from the others in civilisation, and instead we have the plus-de-jouir commanding the subject to work, so that the identifications fall and are replaced by the homogeneous evaluation of capacities, while knowledge, in the place of truth, is activated to lie and, no doubt, to progress as well. One could say that in civilisation these different elements are scattered and that only in psychoanalysis, in pure psychoanalysis, are these elements ordered in discourse.

How, then, do we work when identifications are no longer operating, knowledge is blatantly semblant, and the subjective division is saturated by excess jouissance in the real? In "A Fantasy", Miller concludes with an orientation for analysts – we who are supposed to be "armed against the impasses of civilisation":

> The considerations that I had to skip over would lead us to invert what we say traditionally: the subject supposed to know is the pivot of trans-ference. It seems to me that the last Lacan says something else, he says rather, if I may put it this way: transference is the pivot of the subject supposed to know. In other words, he says that what makes the unconscious *ex-sist* as knowledge is love. Moreover, the question of love, starting with the seminar *Encore*, has provoked special interest, because love is what could effect a medi-ation between the ones-all-alone – and with that in mind, saying that love is imaginary presents some difficulty. This means that the unconscious does not exist. The primary unconscious does not exist as knowledge. For it to become a knowledge, to make it exist as knowledge, love is necessary. And that is why Lacan could say at the end of his seminar *Les non-dupes errent*: a psychoanalysis requires that one love one's unconscious. It is the only way to make the rapport, to establish a rapport

between S_1 and S_2, because in the primary state, we have disjoined Ones, we have scattered Ones. So a psychoanalysis requires that one love one's unconscious in order to make, not the sexual rapport, but the symbolic rapport, exist.[14]

Response to a Question on Identification

First of all I'd like to say that I agree with Rik Loose – identification is always in the register of the Other. It seems to me that throughout his life Lacan asks: "How do we answer the question of Who am I?" He does not want this answer to be in the register of identification. Never. In *Seminar IX* he is busy getting rid of the imaginary dimension of identification, then he introduces identification to the unary trait, but only insofar as it is that which specifies the subject as different from others. So the question of identification is, for Lacan, connected to the question of identity. At the beginning of *Seminar XXIV*, after having listed the three Freudian types of identification, he says that at the end of one's analysis one could identify with one's symptom. I'd like to point out that this phrase "identification with your symptom" was rendered by Jacques-Alain Miller in his commentary on Lacan's very last teaching, *Le Tout Dernier Enseignement*, with the expression *identité sinthomale*, sinthomal identity. Not identification. Not given to you by the Other. What does it mean? It means that it will not be in the register of the signifier. To identify with one's symptom – even though we use nominations in the testimonies, they are not identifications, they are not words given by the Other. They are the name we give ourselves once we have recognised our symptom. Crucially, *the name comes after the effect, it does not produce it.*

At the end of his teaching, Lacan wanted to go further than the unconscious. In *Seminar XXIV* Lacan says that the unconscious is a mental illness that never awakens. Here we are talking about the constant addition of an S_2 to an S_1, the process of the signifying chain constantly interpreting the real: "this happens to me, which means this, this, this..." This is the illness that the unconscious is. It is, of course, useful, as it can amount to the auto-elaboration of a non-standard fiction, producing homeostasis (as Éric Laurent put it in his text "Disruptions of Jouissance"), but Lacan, at this stage of his teaching, is fed up with meaning-making and wants to see if there could be something that could confer an identity on us that would not be of that order.

So in the first instance you need to sever your transferential unconscious from your real unconscious. You need to stop believing that it makes sense. Because it doesn't mean anything. At the end of an analysis it is safe to put the analysand in this position – but not at the beginning, of course. At the end, when meaning has dried up, however, you need to send the subject back to "it doesn't mean anything," it is just a mode of enjoyment that is contingent and singular to that subject. And Lacan's idea, developed by Miller, is that this could be the source of an identity which would not come from the register of the Other. Of course you could not *know* it with knowledge.

When we have gotten rid of all the constructions and elaborations that we came up with in the course of our analysis, we are left with what Freud called the symptomatic residues. With Miller we now call this the sinthome. We are left with this iteration which is absolutely outside meaning, and because our life is rid of all the constructions we have made we can know who (or what, even) we have always been.

We discussed it with Dominique Holvoet during a pass event at the ECF on "Sinthomal Identity": finally I am realising who I have always been – except I could not know it before, because all this other stuff was in the way: my fantasy, my ideals, my identifications. In fact there is something of me that's always been present as this iteration. But it requires that the path be cleared beforehand, so that you can begin to have a know-how about it. I like what Lacan said in *Seminar XXIV*, that a man knows [*connait*] a woman's body, the same word he uses for one's symptom. We need the distinction between *connaissance* and *savoir*. A man does not have knowledge, but he has a *connaissance*, a know-how, of how to be with *this* woman. Not all women, but this particular woman. What will she enjoy? It is the same with one's symptom. It is not *savoir*, not a knowledge woven out of signifiers. It is an intimate *connaissance*. It is a familiarity that we acquire with our symptom once it is free from all the elaborations that we have put in its way. Only when you have this *connaissance*, this kind of familiarity with your symptom, can you begin to know that "it wants this," "it wants that," it pushes you this way and that way – only then can you begin to acquire the know-how to use it. You can begin to orient yourself with it, rather than via meaning. It is not the case that you will gain control over it, no. For example, when I prepare an intervention I cannot do it until the last minute, it has to be *sur le vif*, on the spot, so that it remains alive. It doesn't mean that I procrastinate, or that I am inhibited in relation to working or writing, but that it is an impossible. This is exactly what we want the discourse of the analyst to produce: an impossible. Then you know where it is. It is there. And it is just as well that it's there to anchor you amidst the endless displacement of signifiers. You can gradually acquire a know-how with this sinthome, which Freud was already defining as a foreign body that the body had to learn how to organise itself around. That's the kind of sinthomal identity that we can expect of an analysis taken to its end, one that frees us from identification. You take your grounding, your *connaissance*, from what is real for you, and you teach out of and from that. Of course you have to transform it into some form of knowledge for it to be transmissible.

Concerning the dreams that we have at the end of our analysis, some people say that they come from the real unconscious. I completely disagree – it is still a transferential unconscious, except that the transference now is to psychoanalytic knowledge.

You still produce an elaboration on the eruption of a situation which doesn't mean anything.

Moteriality

At several points during this presentation there was a slip on the word "master signifier" which was enunciated as "matter signifier." So let's end with a few words on this. Matter: what I really want to say is drawn from the last words of Alexandre Stevens' intervention preparing for the NLS Congress, 2021, which includes a quote from Jacques-Alain Miller:

> The event does not bear witness to a truth to be discovered. Rather, it refers to excess, surprise and the contingency of the encounter. It leaves no room for interpretation in terms of meanings. It is therefore about staying away from sense. "Indeed, these are meanings that first present themselves in listening; they are what capture and permeate you. It is already a great deal to succeed in detaching oneself enough from these and to isolate in them the signifiers, and to interpret, on the basis not of signification, but of simple homophony, not of sense but of sound. On occasion, this interpretation can be reduced to making a sound resonate, nothing more.[15]

It is the matter that Lacan was speaking of, the *âme-à-tiers* [*matière*] in *Seminar XXIV*. At the same time it is a joke – *âme-à-tiers* – to get one's soul from a third party, and materiality of the word, *du mot*

– mot-teriality. You seek this mode of jouissance – to ground, to laugh, homophony of language – because *materiel-ne-ment* [matter does not lie, unlike meaning]. Another word play in French. Everything that is not matter, lies. Matter is the only thing you can use to go beyond the lying truth. Your know-how is with your symptom, and it is not in the dimension of language.

Endnotes

Editorial

1 Miller, J.-A., "The Turin Theory of the Subject of the School" (2000), trans. H. Chamberlain and V. Dachy, *Psychoanalytical Notebooks*, No. 33, 2019.

2 Laurent, E., "The Pass and the Guarantee in the School" (1992), trans. P. Dravers and V. Dachy, available online.

3 Lacan, J., "The Founding Act" (1964), trans. J. Mehlman (modified), *Television: A Challenge to the Psychoanalytic Establishment*, ed. J. Copjec, London/New York, Norton, 1990, pp. 97-106.

4 Lacan, J., "Proposition of 9 October 1967 on the Psychoanalyst of the School," trans. R. Grigg, *Analysis*, No. 6, 1995, pp. 1-13.

5 Miller, J.-A., "The Unconscious and the Speaking Body" (2014), trans. A.R. Price *Hurly-Burly*, No. 12, 2015, p. 129.

6 Lacan, J., "Columbia University: Lecture on the Symptom" (1975), trans. A.R. Price and R. Grigg, *Culture/Clinic*, No. 1, 2013, p. 8.

Formation of the Analyst, the End of Analysis

1 Lacan, J., "Proposition of 9 October on the Psychoanalyst of the School", trans. R. Grigg, *Analysis*, No. 6, pp. 1-13; available online.

2 Freud, S., "Analysis Terminable and Interminable" (1937), *S.E.* Vol. XXIII (1937-1939), pp. 209-252, p. 243.

3 Miller, J.-A., "Présentation du thème des Journées de l'ECF 2009: Comment on devient psychanalyste à l'orée du XXIème siècle", *La Lettre mensuelle*, No. 279, June 2009, p. 3.

4 Dupont, L., "La parole vive", delivered at *Question d'École*, Paris, 23 January 2016, published in *La Cause du désir*, No. 92, March 2016, p. 19.

5 Miller, J.-A., *L'Os d'une cure*, Paris, Navarin, 2018, p. 19.

6 Miller, "Présentation...", *op. cit.*, p. 4.

7 Lacan, J., "Joyce the Symptom", trans. A.R. Price, *The Lacanian Review*, No. 5, 2018, p. 14.

8 Miller, *L'Os d'une cure, op. cit.*, p. 50.

9 Miller, J.-A., "Come iniziano le analisi", *La Cause freudienne*, No. 29, February 1995, p. 5.

10 Miller, "Présentation...", *op. cit.*, p. 4.

11 Lacan, J., "Preface to the English-Language Edition of *Seminar XI*" (1976), trans. R. Grigg, *The Lacanian Review*, No. 6, p. 23.

12 Miller, J.-A., "The Unconscious and the Speaking Body", *Hurly-Burly*, No. 12, 2015, p. 126.

13 Miller, *L'Os d'une cure*, *op. cit.*, pp. 29, 28.

14 Miller, "Présentation...", *op. cit.*, p. 4.

15 Miller, *L'Os d'une cure, op. cit.* The following quotes are from pp. 30, 32, 40, 41, 45, 66, 48, 69.

16 Miller, J.-A., "The Unconscious and the Speaking Body", *op. cit.*, p. 131.

17 Miller, "Présentation...", *op. cit.*

18 See "The Unconscious and ...", *op.cit.*, this and the following quotes are from pp. 128-129.

The Rhinoceros and the Desire of the Analyst

1 Available online at https://www.lacan.com/millerlecture.htm

2 Lacan, J., "Intervention à l'EFP le 3 novembre 1973", *Lettres de l'EFP*, No. 15, p. 191.

3 Miller, J.-A., "The Real in the 21st Century", presentation of the theme of the 9th Congress of the WAP (2012), *Hurly-Burly*, No. 9, 2013, p. 206.

4 Laurent, É., "Du réel, faire hazard", *Le Bulletin*, No. 3, ACF, Bordeaux, January 1994.

5 Di Ciaccia, A., "La pratique à plusieurs à l'Antenne 110 de Genval

(Belgique)", available online in Ornicar ? digital, (in French), at WAPOL.org.; cf. Courtil Papers (in English) available online.

Supervision

1 Lacan, J., "Founding Act" (1964), trans. J. Mehlman, *Television: A Challenge to the Psychoanalytic Establishment*, ed. J. Copjec, London/New York, Norton, 1990.

2 Lacan, J., "Discourse à l'École freudienne de Paris" (6 Dec 1967), *Autres écrits*, Paris, Seuil, 2001, p. 266.

3 Lacan, J., "The Direction of the Treatment and the Principles of Its Power" (1958), *Écrits*, trans. B. Fink, London/New York, Norton, 2006.

4 Laurent, É., "On the Right Use of Supervision" (2002), trans. H. Chamberlain, *Psychoanalytical Notebooks*, No. 10, 2003, p. 10.

5 Lacan, J., *Seminar XXIII, The Sinthome* (1975-76), trans. A.R. Price, Cambridge, Polity, 2016.

6 Lacan, J., "Proposition of 9 October 1967 on the Psychoanalyst of the School", trans. R. Grigg, *Analysis*, No. 6, 1995, pp. 1-13. Available online.

7 Lacan, J., *Seminar XXIV, L'insu que sait de l'Une-bévue s'aile à mourre* (1977), unpublished.

8 Lacan, J., "Founding Act", *op. cit.*, p. 97.

From Dreams to Body Event

1 In Spanish, *maldita* means malevolent. From the Latin *maledicens*. The signifier can be divided into: mal (bad) and dita (said). In *Seminar XX, Encore*, at the end of chapter 8, Lacan says, "There is only one way to write

Woman without having to bar it – that is at the level at which woman is truth. And that is why one can only half speak her' (p. 103). She can only be half-said, *mi-dire* in French, which also sounds like médire.

2 Laurent, É., "Interpretation: From Truth to Event", *The Lacanian Review*, No. 8, 2019, pp. 115-132.

3 *Ibid.*

4 Lacan, J., *The Seminar of Jacques Lacan, Book XX, Encore: On Feminine Sexuality, the Limits of Love and Knowledge* (1972-3), ed. J.-A. Miller, trans. B. Fink, London/New York, Norton, 1998, p. 103.

5 Tassara, P., "From the Urgency of an Anxiety to the Urgency of a Satisfaction's Bien-Dire", *The Lacanian Review*, No. 6, 2018, p. 155.

6 Lacan, J., "The Situation of Psychoanalysis and the Training of Psychoanalysts in 1956," *Écrits*, trans. B. Fink, London/New York, Norton, 2006, pp. 384-411.

Present

1 Shanahan F.C., F. "Modes of Presence", *Lacanian Review Online*, 12 April 2020, available online.

2 Ventura, O., *Presentation of the International Fall Seminar of the ELP*, 2020.

3 Lacan, J., *The Seminar of Jacques Lacan, Book XIX, ...or Worse* (1971-2), ed. J.-A. Miller, trans. A.R. Price, Cambridge, Polity, 2018, p. 210.

4 Miller, J.-A., "A Fantasy" (2004), *Psychoanalytical Notebooks*, No. 34, 2019.

5 Cf. Laurent, É., "El sentimiento delirante de la vida" [The Delusional Sense of Life] DIVA, Bs. As., 2011, p. 7.

6 Cf. The notion of 'WellTech': "Wellbeing: the next disrupted industry by tech", by Mirco Pasqualini, 2 January 2020, available online at medium.com.

7 Cf. Laurent, É., *op. cit.*

8 Lacan, J., "The Function and Field of Speech and Language in Psychoanalysis" (1953), *Écrits*, trans. B. Fink, London/New York, Norton, 2006, p. 248.

9 Miller, J.-A., "Le divan. XXI siècle. Demain la mondialisation des divans? Vers le corps portable ", interview by Eric Favereau, 3 July 1999, Libération.fr, available online.

10 Lacan, J., "The Direction of the Treatment and the Principles of Its Power" (1958), *Écrits, op. cit.* p. 516.

11 Lacan, J., "Variations on the Standard Treatment" (1955), *Écrits, op. cit.*, p. 287. "Now, the analyst undoubtedly knows, on the other hand, that he must not respond to appeals that the subject makes to him in this place, as implicit as they may be; otherwise he will see transference love arise there that nothing, except its artificial production, distinguishes from passionate love, the conditions which produced it thus failing due to their effect, analytic discourse being reduced to the silence of the evoked presence."

12 Lacan, J., *The Seminar of Jacques Lacan, Book XI, The Four Fundamental Concepts of Psychoanalysis* (1964), ed. J.-A. Miller, trans. A. Sheridan, London, Penguin, 1979, p. 128.

13 Lacan, J., *The Seminar of Jacques Lacan, Book XX, Encore, The Limits of Love and Knowledge* (1972-3), ed. J.-A. Miller, trans. B. Fink, London/New York, Norton, 1999, p. 152.

14 Laurent, É., "Interpretation: From Truth to Event", argument of the 2020 NLS Congress, trans. P. Dravers and F.F.C. Shanahan, *The Lacanian Review*, No. 8, 2019, p. 116.

15 Shanahan, F.F.C., "To Interpret

Un-corps", Blog of the NLS Congress Ghent 2020, available online.

16 Lacan, J., *Séminaire XXI, Les non-dupes errent*, lesson of 18 December 1973, unpublished.

17 Miller, J.-A., "Jacques Lacan and the Voice" (1988), in *The Later Lacan*, ed. V. Voruz and B. Wolf, Albany NY, State University of New York Press, 2007, pp. 137-146.

18 *Ibid*.

19 Lacan, J., *Le Séminaire livre XVI, D'un Autre à l'autre* (1968-9), Paris, Seuil, 2006.

Bodies Captured by Discourse

1 Lacan, J., *"L'Ombilic du Rêve est un Trou*: Jacques Lacan répond à une question de Marcel Ritter", *La Cause du désir*, No. 102, 2019, pp. 36-37. "C'est du fait d'être né de ce ventre-là et pas d'ailleurs qu'un certain être parlant ou encore ce que j'appelle pour l'instant un parlêtre, ce qui se trouve être une autre définition de l'inconscient, c'est bien d'être né d'un être qui l'a désiré ou pas désiré, mais qui de ce seul fait le situe d'une certaine façon dans le langage, qu'un parlêtre se trouve exclu de sa propre origine."

2 Recordings available via ICLO YouTube channel.

3 Miller, J.-A., "Jouer La Partie" (1990), *La cause du désir*, No. 105, 2020, p. 26.

4 Freud, S., "Inhibitions, Symptoms and Anxiety" (1926), *S.E.* Vol. 20, p. 91, emphasis added.

5 Lacan, J., "Proposition of 9 October on the Psychoanalyst of the School" (1967), trans. R. Grigg, *Analysis*, No. 6, 1995, pp. 1-13.

6 Miller, J.-A., "Milanese Intuitions" (2002), trans. A. Duncan,

Psychoanalytical Notebooks, No. 34, pp. 87, 88.

7 See for example, Chapter 8 of *Seminar XVII*, "From myth to structure". Lacan, J., *The Other Side of Psychoanalysis: The Seminar of Jacques Lacan, Book XVII* (1969-70), ed. J.-A. Miller, trans. R. Grigg, New York/London, Norton, 2007. Quotes are from pp. 124, 120. Cf. also discussion on power and knowledge in *Seminar XVI, D'un Autre à l'autre*, Paris, Seuil, 2006.

8 Miller, "Milanese Intuitions", *op. cit*, p. 122.

9 Foucault, M., "A Preface to Transgression" (1963), *Language, Counter-Memory, Practice: Selected Essays and Interviews*, trans. D.F. Bouchard and S. Simon, ed. D.F. Bouchard, Ithaca NY, Cornell University Press, 1977.

10 cf "Faire passer la jouissance à l'inconscient, c'est-à-dire à la comptabilité...", *Radiophonie*, p. 420.

11 Miller, J.-A., "A Fantasy" (2004), trans. T. Sowley (modified), *Psychoanalytical Notebooks*, No. 34, 2019, pp. 147-8.

12 Miller, "Jouer La Partie", *op. cit*, 2020, p. 28.

13 Miller, "A Fantasy", *op. cit*, p. 148.

14 *Ibid*, pp. 171-2

15 Miller, J.-A., "L'être et l'Un", Lacanian Orientation (2010-2011), course taught under the auspices of the Department of Psychoanalysis, the University of Paris VIII, unpublished, lesson 8.

London Society
of the New
Lacanian School

Individual or institutional online purchases
can be made from our website:

www.londonsociety-nls.org.uk

Printed in Great Britain
by Amazon